MEMORY
&
COMPLICITY

MERCER UNIVERSITY PRESS

Endowed by

TOM WATSON BROWN
and
THE WATSON-BROWN FOUNDATION, INC.

MEMORY
&
COMPLICITY

Poems

Eve Hoffman

Mercer University Press | Macon,Georgia
2018

MUP/ P567

© 2018 by Mercer University Press
Published by Mercer University Press
1501 Mercer University Drive
Macon, Georgia 31207

9 8 7 6 5 4 3 2 1

Books published by Mercer University Press are printed on acid-free paper
that meets the requirements of the American National Standard for
Information Sciences—Permanence of Paper for Printed Library Materials.

ISBN   978-0-88146-659-1
Cataloging-in-Publication Data is available from the Library of Congress

PRINTED IN CANADA

For my grandchildren

Isaac

Howard

Alice

Jacob

Genevieve

and Henry

Contents

Who the poet is, what he or she nominates as a proper theme for poetry, what selves poets discover and confirm through this subject matter—all of this involves an ethical choice. The more volatile the material —and a wounded history, public or private, is always volatile—the more intensely ethical the choice. Poetic ethics are evident and urgent in any culture where tensions between a poet and his or her birthplace are inherited and established.

—Eavan Boland, *Object Lessons*

Foreword

Memories are like poetry. We don't remember events in our lives in perfect narrative; they arise in glimpses, images, snippets of expressions from captured moments. Memories are fragments of time. Sometimes they emerge as bits of story, other times only impressions. *I remember my father's sense of humor* may not evoke any particular instance, but a general sense of a life lived.

Neuroscientists tell us that each time we bring a memory back to consciousness, we alter its details slightly. Memories evolve and change; all memories are altered memories. The personal truth of a memory therefore lies in the emotions it arouses, not the details, which we may revise over time to reflect our desires. Poetry like that in *Memory & Complicity* weaves the fragile tendrils of our recollections into emotional coherence, and so captures the evocative truths of memory.

Eve Hoffman's poetry is memoir made lyrical. *Memory & Complicity* unfolds as an intensely personal story, scenes from a life sometimes epic, sometimes intimate. We never doubt that it is one woman's story, the details and peculiarities of growing up in Georgia, on a family farm, caught in the time-flow of the second half of the 20th century. It is all the more remarkable, then, how often we discover our own stories in hers. Eve's poetry speaks to our common experience, even for those of us not brought up in the south, whose parents would never dream of having a housekeeper eat from separate dishes, who did not wake up each morning to the mooing of cows or eat farm-grown pork, or who were steeped in the lore Eve laments having missed— Israel, the Holocaust, Yiddish and lox.

Memories are like poetry. *She runs towards us, a ten year-old girl in pigtails.* We all have known that girl, and we smile inwardly, whether the memory of her is in West Philadelphia or Oakland or Mobile or a farm on the outskirts of Atlanta, Georgia. Eve's memories transform our own, both those we share with her (whatever they are—Tonka toys or Chopin's Preludes, Billie Holliday's *Strange Fruit* or the first fireflies of summer) and those that we do not (whatever they are—hog slaughtering or houseboats in Sausalito, the associations of a Yellow Dress or red Georgia clay). If every memory brought up is a memory altered, and is ultimately about emotional truth, reading *Memory & Complicity* involves merging some of our own memories into Eve's, amending slightly our inner biographical narrative to absorb Eve's passion for her childhood into recollections of our own.

Poetry forges a direct line to the heart. *Memory & Complicity* touches us that way, evoking nostalgia for a childhood home or the joy of a new love, the excitement of first sex or the grief of loss. The beauty of this deeply autobiographical collection is how Eve uses poetic forms to take us there, travelling through her story, beside her.

On that journey, Eve confronts our moral sensibilities. Being a white, Jewish girl (and then woman) of privilege in the South over the last half-century was fraught with contradictions and challenge. Eve reveals not being taught of the 1906 Atlanta race riot, or of her great-grandmother's involvement in the Georgia Women's Suffrage movement. She recalls black field hands not being invited to sit at a common table, and of learning the startling truth that lynchings were not the furtive acts of rednecks but public displays of racial power where tickets were sometimes sold. She shares the experience of living on a farm where cows were shot and hung by their legs to be butchered. In her honest, unembellished way, Eve's unsettling glimpses of her own past are a moral challenge to our own willful ignorances and the difficult truths of our own life history.

Eve's poetry is thus not only about memory, but complicity. It tells of a man dying of AIDS—her partner Sal's brother—body wracked with sores, seeking solace from a church that was willing to grant it only in death. It is about *Whites Only* water fountains and girls who *don't need* to learn to read. A cold father and a mother who keeps confidence with her daughter's first need for sanitary napkins. Lynching nooses and segregated buses and postcards of beaten Negroes. The Temple bombing and the Holocaust and swastikas carved into tables. And the quotidian complicities of living life—selling a farm, selling a home, finally repurposing a barn that still held the spirit of her beloved husband, Howard—the guilt of moving on. Eve shows us we are all complicit, we must be, because we are all burdened with the responsibility of our choices, even of the hard choices, and even of the choices others make, or the ones that we inherit. We are complicit in the very act of living in an imperfect, unjust world.

One of the beauties of *Memory & Complicity* is that Eve negotiates us through these troubling images and memories without getting preachy or maudlin. They are woven through the flow of her life along with lessons on cooking and the simplicities of childhood, courtship and marriage, flowers and friends and family. The art of *Memory & Complicity* is not only in the poetry itself, but in the artistry of its organization; it portrays a life complete.

Poetry is like memory. It stays with us, reappearing at moments of quiet, populating our imaginations, dotting our lives with color. *Memory & Complicity* reminds us of the joy of each moment and the sadnesses of years. Through the beauty of Eve's verse, each of us grew up on Neely Farm, a vividly real imaginary place where we reached out and began touching life, and where we were touched in return by it, *running barefoot in summer rain, bits of fresh cut grass sticking between our toes.*

—Paul Root Wolpe, Ph.D.
Director, Center for Ethics, Emory University

PROLOGUE

~ top left window, my bedroom ~

Sign of the Times

My mother canning green beans and beets. My brothers and I forbidden
to walk past the stove—the pressure cooker might explode. White flight
and *seg* academies for white parents who refused to send their children
to integrated schools. A cousin buying what he believed to be a Cherokee-made
treasure at the Cherokee reservation in North Carolina. When he got home,
found *Made in Japan* stamped on the bottom. The doomsday nuclear clock
ticking down on the cover of the *Bulletin of Atomic Scientists*. My mother
and grandfather disagreeing about nuclear power. He imagining nuclear medicine;
she imagining the bomb. Black-faced yard jockeys in other people's front yards.

Red Clay

Skirts of summer dust trailing bicycles on dirt roads,
Guernsey and Holstein calves sucking children's fingers,
red-tailed hawks teaching fledglings to fly,
hide-and-seek between damp sheets on the clothesline.

Fields of crimson clover bending with the wind,
'coon hounds baying on full moon nights,
alfalfa hay bales filling haylofts,
hog-killing after first frost—chitlins and cracklings.

Whites Only signs over water fountains,
on bathroom doors and restaurants,
pine trees snapping during ice storms,
rows of icicles hanging along whitewashed fences.

Tire swings dangling from the limb
of a hundred-year-old oak tree,
red clay-stained pants and socks,
Yellow Tonka dump trucks in the sand pile.

The smell of Mother's perfume—
        I wish I could remember its name.

I

~ my brothers hiding at the top of the stairs, jumping out to scare me ~

Birthright

1.

I come from the rush of a flushed covey of quail,
from summer songs of tree frogs, bullfrogs,
and great horned owls, from being frightened
by the shrill call of a tiny screech owl,
from the year a murder of crows ate all the corn seed
in the fifty-acre bottomlands and it had to be replanted,
from whip-poor-will calls at dusk.

I come from a field of daffodils as far as a child's eye could see,
from learning to find Orion's Belt, the Big Dipper,
and Sagittarius in the night sky,
from walking in the woods with my mother
as she pointed out mayapple, trillium, bloodroot,
hepatica, Solomon's seal and maidenhair fern,
from leaving windows open on summer nights,
closing them in the morning to keep the cool air inside,
from banking the fireplaces last thing before bed in winter.

2.

I come from my braids so tight they hurt,
from riding bicycles barefoot, from clinging
to a runaway horse hell-bent for the barn;
I come from fingers stained blue-black while blackberry-picking,
long-sleeved shirts and yellow sulfur power to protect from chiggers,
calamine lotion for poison ivy, violent gentian on cuts and scrapes,
from always having dogs—Snuggybangs, Zeus, Dinah—
I've forgotten most of their names.
I come from curry-combing horses, picking stones
out of their hooves, cleaning saddles and bridles
with saddle soap, rubbing the tack with linseed oil,
from the acrid smell of urine-soaked hay when
mucking out horse stalls, from piano lessons,
from the perfume of milk and manure in a dairy barn.
I come from watching a cow get shot in the forehead,
then jerked up by a rope on its hind legs to hang

from the limb of an oak tree before being butchered.

3.

I come from segregated buses and schools,
from a home where *the n-word* was forbidden,
making fun of someone handicapped was forbidden,
having your mouth washed out with Ivory soap
was punishment for either. I come from a drawer
of separate dishes for the maid to use when she ate.
I come from the woods on fire and my mother
driving me and my brothers across the farm
taking Hershey bars *for energy* to the men
fighting to keep the fire out of a wheat field—
the Hershey bars melting before they could be opened,
the men's black skin dripping, shiny with sweat.

I come from my grandparents hosting veterans
and locally-stationed military at barbeque-and-beer suppers—
whole pigs cooking all night in an earthen pit
by *Negro* veterans returned from World War II to plow
and plant alfalfa and corn, bail hay, and blow silage—
but they were not invited to sit at the table,
ate standing, holding their plates by the hot open pit.

4.

I come from a Jewish household in which we ate
farm-grown pork, except on Friday nights
and during Passover, Rosh Hashanah, and Yom Kippur.
I come from southern accents but no Hebrew or Yiddish,
no bagels or lox, *latkes* or *kugel* on our table,
from an elementary school principal who told
my brother Nathan she was worried our family
would go to Hell because we didn't believe in Jesus.

I come from not knowing my great-grandmother
was secretary of the Georgia Women's Suffrage movement,
from never learning about the 1906 Atlanta race riot,
about the lynching of *Negroes*, or the 1915 mob lynching

in Marietta, Georgia of Leo Frank, the Jewish
superintendent in a pencil factory,
I come from being unaware of the Holocaust, of Israel,
being unfamiliar with the word *anti-Semitic*—even though
my brother was chased at Dunwoody Elementary,
shoved against a wall by another student who believed
that, because he was Jewish, he was the devil
and that he had horns to prove it.

       5.

I come from my brothers hiding at the top of the stairs,
jumping out to scare me, from listening to Tallulah Bankhead,
Fibber McGee and Molly, and The Great Gildersleeve
broadcast from the small brown Motorola radio on top of the icebox
while we washed and dried Sunday supper dishes.
I come from the sweet scent and smooth feel
of my mother's golden glycerin Pears soap,
from Guernsey cream so thick you'd have to spoon it,
from catching lightning bugs, putting them
into a Mason jar with holes punched in the lid;
I come from tying a thread to the leg of a June bug,
watching it fly round and round in circles
trying to break free.

Miss Lizzie's Kitchen

Turnip greens, green beans, green tomatoes
in the garden just outside Miss Lizzie's screen door,
Mason jars full of yellow-orange peaches,
dense purple-red beets, bread and butter pickles;
slow-cooked chicken dripping from the bone—
she'd raised the chicken, wrung its neck,
watched it flap and flop all over the yard,
blood soaking the ground. Her father took her
out of school at age ten, put her to work
in the Georgia fields—
   Girls don't need to learn to read.

Sweet acrid collards, creamed corn,
Big Boy and beefsteak tomatoes.

Once Georgia law allowed *Negroes* to register to vote,
Miss Lizzie never missed an election.
In Sunday best, hair freed from the rag she tied
around it during the week and braided into a crown,
she rode to the polls with my mother Rachel
who wore gathered skirts and tailored blouses,
a soft bun at the nape of her neck.
Ages identical, skin colors and stations distinct,
these women called one another *Sister,*
shared five decades of secrets—
   I'm gonna take what I know to the grave,
    so jus' don't ask,
but at eighty-five she told me of the day
she stood between my mother's parents,
sent them to separate rooms until
they made peace—no other details;
she told me of anger, still, with her father
for cutting short her education—
   I could have been something!

Chestnuts freed from porcupine burrs,
sweet potato pies cooling on the windowsill.

Warmth flooded Miss Lizzie's winter kitchen,
tiny beads of sweat lined her summer brow.
She was one-eighth Cherokee, but we were warned
never to mention her Indian heritage—
she'd been taught that *Indian blood is dirty*.
We wondered if that one-eighth accounted
for her acute hearing, her dead-eye shot
with a .22 Remington rifle.

Every so often Miss Lizzie'd come by the house—
    Can I borrow a little change?
always for someone else—for bail, for brakes,
a funeral, a back-alley abortion or to repair one.
We knew better than to ask, or to mention her husband
who'd succumbed to syphilis before I was born.

Black-eyed peas shelled in a white enameled pot,
butter rounds crosshatched with a knife handle,
a black iron skillet of steaming corn bread.

Rachel's Pot

In this pot she simmered blackberries
into jam, scorching sweetness
filling half-pint Mason jars.
My brothers and I scraped
the semi-hardened black nectar
stuck to the sides and bottom of the pot,
let it melt on our tongues.

In this pot she turned rock-hard bitter quince
from the tree by the gravel driveway
into gooey strips, sweet candy jam,
and pears from the gnarled tree
in the backyard into amber preserves.
In this pot she boiled ten ears of sweet corn at a time,
fifteen minutes stalk to table;
blanched double handfuls of string beans
to a burst of green, dumped them into an ice bath
to stop the cooking—exactly like
the county Home Demonstration Agent had taught her—
layered them in white plastic quart boxes
with red lids, stacked the boxes
in our first-ever freezer in the basement—

       and then my mother walked outside, barefoot,
       leaned down and picked a four-leaf clover,
       sometimes two.

Learning to Float

My brothers and I learned to swim in a spring-fed pond—
bulrushes at one end, at the other,
an arbor with something green climbing all over it
where our grandmother would stand
fishing for bass and bream—wide brimmed straw hat
and sling-back espadrille heels with open toes.

When we waded into the pond,
mud covered our ankles,
sticky, stinky, gooey between our toes.
We learned to float first,
our mother in a celadon wool bathing suit
that always smelled like pond scum
and never dried completely,
instructed us—
> Arch your back, toes near the surface.
> Relax. Tilt your head back.
> Ignore the cold springs.

Floating was about safety—
> If you get a cramp,
> turn on your back and float.
It was about lying suspended in the water
trusting turtles, snakes and frogs
were more afraid of us than we were of them,
about not panicking when fish nibbled
the moles on our legs, about lambs and
horses and bearded men in the clouds,
about twisting our bodies
to watch kingfishers dive
and dragonflies scoot jaggedly
just above the surface.

Floating was about my mother's hands
in the water just below my back,
        knowing she would catch me
        if I began to sink.

Circles in the Sky

What did I know of war—
a girl of eight or ten on a dairy farm bordered
by a winding river with an Indian name I couldn't spell,
green terraced pastures cascading from red clay hills.
Children wore dog tags embossed
with name, address, and date of birth—
grey metal rectangles, rounded at the corners,
a small *v* notched at one end to hold your teeth apart
if you were dead. Mine hung around my neck
on a chain of tiny balls like the pull chains on lights.

I knew savings bond booklets, twenty-five cent stamps
pasted into squares until the total
was $18.75 and would mature into $25.00.
I knew air-raid drills, duck and cover exercises
under school desks, lining up along school hall walls,
crouching with arms on top of our heads,
as if our thin arms and small hands could protect us.
I knew fighter pilots from the Chamblee Naval Air Station
tracing the river because the topography resembled Korea—
somewhere so distant we children could not imagine.
They'd swoop up, dive down, cut their engines, and glide.
We'd hold our breath until the engines restarted
and the planes turned skyward again.

I knew Uncle Joel, a hero in the Pacific, ravaged
by war and dysentery coming home weighing
ninety-seven pounds. He continued to be called
Colonel after he became a lawyer and practiced
in Atlanta with my father. On birthdays he'd give me
a dollar for each year of my age until my father
told him to stop. Uncle George, a dentist
and also a colonel, never mentioned military rank—
a back brace sufficient reminder of his jeep rolling
at the Battle of the Bulge. We could feel it
when we hugged him. Neither uncle had children,

no cousins with whom to trade family stories.

What did I know of war
watching silver specks leave contrail circles
in the blue sky, certain those circles
were the size of bombs, that they marked
the place from which bombs would drop—

        barefoot child on summer days
        picking blue cornflowers beside the ditch.

Mother/Daughter

I remember, as a child of nine or ten, standing on a chair,
taking the four-inch-thick Webster's Dictionary
from the wall of floor-to-ceiling bookshelves
in our living room and looking up the words
      pregnant and *penis,*
finding these words daring, exciting,
then shoving the heavy dictionary back into place
when I'd hear Mother in her Dr. Scholl's sandals
crossing the oriental rug into the room.

      I remember her summer gathered skirts
      and pastel tailored blouses.

I remember pulling her wrapped-in-toilet-paper
used Kotex out of the trashcan in the bathroom,
opening the package to examine its contents,
      dried blood turning brown.
I closed it quickly, rewrapped it as neatly
as I could, placed it in the bottom of the trashcan
so she might not notice it had been moved.

      I remember how she'd pull her long brown hair
      into a loose bun and secure it with two hairpins.

I remember Kotex ads with models in daytime suits and dresses
      Not a shadow of doubt. . . .
and Modess ads with models in Dior-esque evening gowns—
      Modess. . .because
and discovering I'd gotten my period
one summer Sunday afternoon at my grandparents' house.
Mother drove me home for my *supplies*—
sanitary napkins and the white elastic belt
with which to hold them in place. She promised
that when we returned she'd not tell anyone why we'd left.

I remember picking baskets of daffodils with her—
Barrett Brownings, Butter and Eggs, King Alfreds.

I remember hiding with one of my brothers
in a hayloft above the horses, watching dogs mate.
They'd been put together in a pen across the yard,
got stuck together—facing in opposite directions
for what seemed an interminable length of time.
I climbed down the ladder, ran hollering
      Mother, the dogs are stuck together!
She turned the hose on the dogs,
shocking them into jerking apart.

      I remember her beds of tulips along our driveway—
      Queen of Nights, Sky High Scarlets, La Courtines.

I remember watching the *breeder man*,
artificial insemination purveyor for the dairy herd,
speeding down the dirt road, leaving a wall of dust.
to catch a cow during her sanding heat
which would last only a few hours.
Methodically, he'd put on a rubber glove that went
all the way to his arm pit, lift the cow's tail
and stick his arm completely inside of her,
where he'd break a small vial of bull semen,
chosen in hopes of breeding improved quality
into the Holstein and Guernsey dairy herd.

      I remember the stain on Mother's fingertips
      after she'd applied rouge, her only makeup.

I remember a hot summer afternoon,
my seventh-grade graduation party
in the center of an open farm field—
all eleven of us in the class played spin-the-bottle
using an empty green-glass Coca-Cola bottle.
Impatient with the time it took to spin the bottle,
we invented clockwise/counterclockwise circles

of boys and girls kissing one another in turn.
After my classmates left, I went guiltily to my room.
Mother came upstairs, sat on the edge of my bed, asked
          What's the matter?
She assured me that kissing boys was not a bad thing.
I came down for supper.

          I remember her elegant suit of geometric reds and purples—
          fine-wool fabric designed by her friend Pola Stout in New York.

I remember finding *balloons* in my father's bedside table,
and sometimes hearing the soft thud of a chairback being shoved
up under the handle of my mother and father's bedroom door
so none of us could come in. Why do I think I remember
that the *balloons* were orange?

          I remember her singing Brahms' *Lullaby* at night.

I remember Mother telling my eight-year-old brother
to run across the farm and find Neal—a *colored* man
who worked on the farm but began and ended each day
in a chauffeur's uniform, driving my father
(who didn't drive and we never knew why)
to and from his law office twenty miles away—
telling my brother to ask Neal to come quickly,
to take her to the doctor. I remember
Mother climbing into the backseat of the car,
a towel beneath her soaking up blood.
Neal in the driver's seat.

          At six, I had no idea what a miscarriage was.

I remember Mother teaching me how to poach an egg
and to cut out grapefruit sections using a small knife curved at the tip.
I remember discovering something mysterious
in her underwear drawer—something that wasn't bras,
panties, garter belts, or Hanes stockings.
(Why I was poking around in her drawers I don't remember,

but I can still smell the sachet she used.)
I confessed my discovery to her, have no memory
of how she explained to me her douche bag.

     I remember the rings she wore after her divorce—
     amethyst, opal, and turquoise.

I remember Mother's brown hair cascading
half-way down her back, silvering at the temples.
I remember her in long nightgowns
brushing her hair and braiding it into a single braid

     just before bedtime.

The Yellow Dress

Atlanta, Georgia, October 1958

I loved this dressy-dress
as I spun round and round
in the dressing-room mirror
of Rich's Department Store—
swirling the skirt, checking it out,
front, back, side-to-side—
yellow chiffon, scooped neck,
puffed sleeves, starched crinolines
two-toned crisscrossed green sash.

My mother used the store telephone to call
my father, an attorney in his office
a few blocks away, to come see the dress
and pay for it. He refused.
   It's too expensive for a sixteen-year-old girl.

Mother and I took the escalators
to Rich's fifth-floor executive offices
where Mimi, my mother's father,
pulled from his gold money clip
fifty dollars in new bills
—he always had crisp money—
and handed it to my mother.

   ~

The first time I wore the yellow dress
was for my installation as president
of The Temple Youth Group during
the fall membership party in the synagogue social hall—
a plain boxy room we'd decorated
with ribbons of colored crepe paper,
a banner reading *Let's Break All Membership Records,*
and black construction paper 45 RPM records,

names of current hits printed across them—
The Purple People Eater, *All You Have to Do Is Dream*,
and *Catch a Falling Star*.

I felt pretty—really, really pretty.

~

Five hours after the Youth Group party ended,
while I lay asleep in my bedroom,
the yellow dress across a chair,
a trail of stockings and dyed-to-match
yellow shoes on the floor,
The Temple was bombed—
a gaping hole blasted
in the north side of the building
where just hours before we'd been dancing
to Elvis Presley, Perry Como, and the Kingston Trio—
walls of the offices and religious school classrooms blown out,
stained-glass windows shattered,
dust and shards of plaster from elaborate
friezes representing the twelve tribes of Israel
scattered across the sanctuary pews and floor,
and construction paper 45 RPM records
strewn among broken brick and concrete.

~

Five men with histories of anti-Semitic and racist
associations were arrested within a few days—
George Bright, Kenneth Griffin, Luther Corley,
brothers Robert and Richard Bolling—
all were indicted for setting off fifty sticks of dynamite
in the recessed side entry of The Temple—
dynamite supplied by J. B. Stoner,
founder and chairman of the National States Rights Party
who was out of town at the time of the bombing.

Bright, a thirty-four-year-old cotton mill engineer,
the probable mastermind, was first to be tried—
represented by, among others, James R. Venable,
Imperial Wizard of the National Knights of the Ku Klux Klan.
his first trial ended in a hung jury;
his second in an acquittal.
Discouraged prosecutors dropped charges
against the other men indicted

for bombing the synagogue
my great-grandparents helped found in 1867,
the synagogue where my grandparents were married,
where my mother had been confirmed,
the congregation whose Rabbi, Jacob Rothschild,
was active in the Civil Rights Movement,

the congregation where I had just become
president of The Temple Youth Group.

~

Twenty years and dozens of loved dresses later,
I come across the yellow dress
on a wire hanger in the chifforobe
in my childhood room in my mother's house.
I throw it across my arm, take it home,
hang it in the guest room closet.

One morning, looking for extra pillows in the closet,
I pull out the yellow dress,
hold it up against my body,
twirl round and round in front of the mirror.
I can feel the sideways sway of *slow dancing*,
the hand of a teenage boy at my waist.

I can hear the Platters singing
Smoke Gets in Your Eyes.

In the Bottomlands

From a Neely Farm photograph

She runs towards us,
a ten year-old girl in pigtails,
boy's horizontal-striped T-shirt
covering her flat chest,
a flowered skirt flying out to her side,
brown lace-up shoes and white socks—
the right sock slipping down to her ankle.

She runs, skips along a farm road
past oak, hickory and pine trees canting towards
a field of stubs where silage corn has been cut,
past the banks of the Chattahoochee River
which floods this bottomland twice a year
scaring her when the brown river water slips up the hill
close to one of the farmhand's houses.
Her mother tells her not to worry
about their home further up the hill—
> *If the water gets that high,*
> *the whole city of Atlanta will be flooded.*

She runs with the sun in her face,
behind her, a wooden gate ajar—three boards high,
a fourth on the diagonal steadies it.
She doesn't wonder why her father, a successful attorney
with his name in gold on his frosted-glass office door,
shops only in the bargain basement
of Rich's Department Store, why he buys
the same things for her and her two brothers.
She'll wear boys' shirts all through elementary school,
a brown bomber jacket in winter. She doesn't know
that on her sixteenth birthday her mother
will buy her the red coat she's always wanted.
For now, she worries about when she'll get to have
a bra and to wear bright red Revlon lipstick—

Fire & Ice or *Persian Melon?*

She loves her grandmother Bama's Floating Island—
egg custard from scratch, meringue floating on top;
she gags when her other grandmother, Bobo, makes
gefilte fish—whole carp, pike, and whitefish flopping
in the sink waiting to be filleted and ground
but she's fascinated when Bobo braids *challah* dough
with three strands, just like her own pigtails.

She believes the noises she hears at night
in her bedroom ceiling are snakes crawling,
not squirrels playing chase. She thinks about
Madame Alexander dolls, Girl Scout badges,
and the 4-H prize she wins for sewing a white four-gored skirt
with green 4-H clovers stenciled on each gore.
She feels guilty when her horse Duke dies
while she's away at summer camp—believes he died
because she didn't ride him often enough.

She hasn't imagined the first time she'll wear
stockings—a new pair of her mother's held up

just below her knees with rubber bands.
She'll be going to the Metropolitan Opera in Atlanta;
her photo with her parents will be on the front page
of the next morning's *Atlanta Constitution*.
She hasn't imagined looking at her face in the mirror
the morning after she's had sex for the first time—
and finding it unchanged.

She runs toward us unaware
that, while her mother was pregnant with her,
Jewish children in Europe were being murdered;
that her parents will divorce after twenty years of marriage;
that a month after she graduates from college three young men
will be murdered for registering *Negroes* to vote
and buried under a Mississippi dam,

that she will become a widow at fifty-two.

She runs toward us,
her braids flying, arms flying, skirt flying—
long before guilt and grief,
      long before she'll need steadying.

~ complained about whose turn it was to feed the dogs and rabbits ~

She—Part One

She was a scaredy-cat,
afraid of howling winds tossing back tin roofs,
coonhounds braying on full-moon Georgia nights,
snakes, all of them, not just the copperheads.
She was a goody-two-shoes—
straight A's, never got a speeding ticket,
never lied about where she was.

At Smith College she was intimidated
by her classmates with monogrammed pinky rings,
a cappella voices, and AP credits,
who read the *New York Times* every day.
She never skipped class,
never turned in a paper late,
believed she wasn't smart enough
to raise her hand and answer faculty questions.

On her eighteenth birthday she registered to vote,
never missed voting but was not political—
skipped John Kennedy at Amherst
and Martin Luther King at Smith—told her friends,
I can hear Dr. King at home in Atlanta anytime.
She didn't participate
in the 1963 March on Washington
but spent a summer in Africa
(not a thing southern white girls did)
with a professor and a group of college students—
exchanged the vitriol of Alabama's George Wallace
for the bile of Southern Rhodesia's Ian Smith
clawing to maintain white colonial control.

She never got drunk,
never slipped a bottle of Chianti
into her dorm room.
She was ashamed that her parents were divorcing
after twenty years of marriage,
never mentioned it to anyone in college.

After Smith graduation, she drove
her yellow 1964 Chevy Impala
cross-country to San Francisco—
her one contact, a temporary place
to sleep in a Gough Street Victorian house
with a Berkeley graduate
from an East Bay family whose politics ran
pro-Goldwater and anti-Voting Rights Act,
an artist who painted Hawaiian oceanscapes
and whose father was General at the Presidio,
a student who told stories about
her mother's relationship with Tom Wolfe,
and a sub-continent Indian who wore
not-gaudy-but-extremely-large
rubies, sapphires, and diamonds.
They invited her to stay on permanently.

She wore her long hair in a French twist,
every strand in place, dark eye shadow,
as was the fashion, shoes and handbags matching.
For five years she drove Highway 101 forty miles
each way to Stanford, where she worked
as a *secretary*— coordinating authors and editors
for books on colonialism in Africa,
advising African studies Ph.D. candidates,
curating an Africana collection
of books and ephemeral materials.
She took piano lessons on her lunch hour,
shared coffee breaks with visiting scholars—
Theodore Draper, Barbara Tuchman,
and a charming Czech whose anti-Communist
paranoia she came to understand after learning
he had watched the Communists
hang his father in a public square.

~

Six months after arriving in San Francisco
she walked into a friend's kitchen on 22nd Avenue
holding the friend's new baby in her arms.
A six foot tall man, sawdust highlights in his curls,
came down the ladder from where he'd been helping
the baby's father level new cabinets,
pointed to the baby, looked at her and said,
You should have a dozen like that,
picked up a tool and climbed back up the ladder.

Two weeks later the man with sawdust curls called,
Hey, I've just cooked duck à l'orange
here at our friends' house on 22nd.
Why don't you come and join us?
To which she replied, *I've just driven*
forty miles in rush-hour traffic.
If you want me to join you, come pick me up.

He drove to Gough Street to get her—
and, once he'd found his way there,
came often to pick her up at the Victorian house.
They shared hamburgers at Hippo's,
turkey legs at Tommy's Joynt,
danced waltzes and polkas at the San Francisco
symphony Black and White ball,
hiked Mount Tam, sailed to Monterey Bay
(which is when she discovered that seasickness
in Pacific Ocean swells is a real thing).
One sunny afternoon, he jumped off
the Hyde Street cable car, sprinted
to the front of the line at Swensen's Ice Cream,
bought a vanilla cone, raced the cable car
back up the hill, jumped on, handed her
the ice cream cone to the cheers of other riders.

He lived on a houseboat
permanently moored in Sausalito—
his décor: Rex Stout mysteries, Plato's *Republic*,

George Washington and Moss Hart biographies,
and two telephone poles on the dock,
which he used to train for tossing the caber
at the Northern California Highland Games.
He introduced her to the elders of Muir Woods,
the surf of Big Sur, Irish coffee at the Buena Vista,
the tunneled Wawona sequoia at Yosemite,
spider monkeys gallivanting and teasing
on Monkey Island at the San Francisco Zoo.
Every so often he'd turn to her, tell her,
I'm going to marry you—
not in any pushy way, just as a matter of fact.
One evening her housemate from the East Bay
confided to her (a second glass of wine in her hand)
I know you're Jewish, too, but he is _too_ Jewish.
He isn't good enough for you.
Shortly afterward she was asked to move out.

She rented an apartment on Divisadero Street,
the first time in her life she'd lived alone—
bought a set of shrink-wrapped
Noritake plates and bowls at the Emporium
and eight glasses at Cost Plus.
She used empty Campbell soup cans
with the labels torn off for candlesticks,
spent lots more time with the *too Jewish* man.
A few months later on a chilly Sunday afternoon
at the zoo, fog rolling in,
a bride-white peacock strutting and preening
in the midst of a muster of blue-green ones in front of them,
he reminded her again *I am going to marry you.*
This time, she turned to him and said, *Yes!*

His Connecticut family was thrilled.
Members of her Georgia family
felt compelled to investigate him—after all,
they hadn't known *his people* for generations,
he was thirteen years older than she,

previously briefly married, not a doctor
or a lawyer, no college diploma,
(let alone an Ivy League one),
was catholic in his culinary and literary tastes,
generous with bear hugs and laughter—
uncommon currencies in her family

A few weeks before their wedding,
her mother called from Georgia—
All I've learned is he's had a few speeding tickets
and is legally divorced in Nevada.
I don't know if this marriage is right or wrong,
but I will support you all the way.

Six days before the wedding,
she answered the phone in her office—
her lawyer father was calling from D.C.
(He'd previously refused to attend the wedding
because his second wife was not to be included
in the bridal party receiving line.)
I want to advise you that you will be charged
with bigamy the morning after your wedding.

~

The wedding was held in her mother's backyard
where she'd grown up climbing an apple tree,
picking rock-hard pears her mother turned into jam,
standing on a swing pumping as high as possible.
Her older brother walked her out the back door,
past the clothesline with white clematis
wrapping its poles, to a *chuppah* under the trees—
Handel's *Water Music* for the processional,
Royal Fireworks for the recessional
as she and her husband walked down
a yellow zinnia-lined path through
the vegetable garden to supper and dancing
on an abandoned tennis court—

in each corner vertical bundles of dried farm corn stalks
held together with wide amber satin ribbons.

Years later she learned that a family friend,
Mr. Smith, ex-FBI, had stood guard
during the wedding in case of any disruption.

~

She and her husband returned to San Francisco—
sailing with friends in the Bay,
the boat heeling, sails skimming the water;
running two miles every morning
in Golden Gate Park,
drinking too much aquavit and elephant beer
with Danish friends,
joining an anti–Vietnam war march
behind a gaggle of nuns,
sitting side-by-side on the San Francisco wharf
eating Dungeness crabs,
tossing shells to passing gulls,
sharing a loaf of warm Boudin sourdough bread,
drinking cold Anchor Steam beer.
She wore miniskirts and braids on weekends,
a beaded band across her forehead.

One afternoon her husband sailed her package
of birth control pills off the back deck
of their second-floor apartment—
but month after month her menstrual period
continued to come. Her doctor explained
that her fallopian tubes were blocked;
she'd never be able to get pregnant.
On the street, she'd look away
from women pushing strollers and carriages,
turn away from small children
laughing on slides and swings in parks.
She felt like a Biblical *barren woman*.

After three years they moved back to a cottage
on the Georgia dairy farm where she'd grown up;
he built them a home with his own hands.
Her mother recommended a new doctor.
She gave birth to a son, had a miscarriage,
gave birth to a daughter, another miscarriage,
gave birth to a second daughter, had her tubes tied.

She drove carpools to Montessori and Girl Scouts,
roller-blade hockey and religious school.
He helped high school students
build homecoming floats.
She made scratch granola and raisin-bran muffins,
birthday cakes with ceramic animal decorations.
He wove stories for their children
of the Tweedie-Dum-Dinkums—
purple socks and orange underwear,
blue pointed shoes turning up at the toes,
tiny wings to fly horizontally and vertically.
Their children did homework
with a modicum of fuss,
played soccer on Saturdays,
competed on summer swim teams
throughout north Georgia,
complained about whose turn it was
to feed the dogs and rabbits.

She served on the board of Zoo Atlanta,
became president of the League of Women Voters.
He chaired the board of Big Brothers/Big Sisters,
the Department of Family and Children's Services,
encouraged her to run for the Board of Education,
made her stand in the kitchen and practice
asking people to vote for her
so that in 105-degree summer heat,
wearing stockings and heels,
she could confidently knock on strangers' doors

and ask them to vote for her.
She defeated the incumbent,
made bond rating presentations in New York—
dark blue suit, white silk blouse, pearls, navy pumps.
She was honored by Smith College
as a *Remarkable Woman*.
He told her, *You can do anything you set your mind to*
and danced her around the kitchen.

~

Frozen Friday February night, two in the morning.
He collapses onto the concrete driveway just outside
the emergency room of St. Joseph's Hospital.
Doctors insert a pacemaker;
the chaplain brings her a blanket and pillow—
as if she could sleep in the waiting room.

Four nights, four mornings, four days come and go.
Their eighteen year old daughter,
a high school senior, skips classes;
their twenty-one year old daughter flies home
from competing in a college swim meet in Ohio;
their son, twenty-three, home on a graduate school break,
cancels his return to Connecticut.
She wears her dead mother's coat to the hospital,
sleeps under it on the floor outside
the cardiac care unit,
as if her mother is holding her.

Family and friends appear
from Florida, California, Alaska, New York,
from Minnesota and from around the corner—
keep company with her and their children
in the halls, the coffee shop, the bathrooms,
wandering from waiting room to waiting room,
pacing the parking lot in the icy cold,
taking turns keeping her husband company

in a dusky room of beeps and hums,
tubes and plastic bags dripping liquids.

Day five. Mid-morning. Two doctors usher her,
their children, and close family into a softly lit room
with comfortable sofas, tasteful pastel prints
on the walls, boxes of Kleenex on the coffee table
alongside bouquets of silk flowers.
> *His organs are failing.*
> *Even if a heart valve transplant worked,*
> *he would have no quality of life.*

A friend calls their Rabbi.

~

She and her children hole up in a cold steel stairwell
twenty yards from where her husband lies.
Machines and IVs run their course,
begin to be unplugged—
only enough morphine drip and oxygen
to keep him comfortable.
They decide to bury him in Connecticut
beside his parents and grandparents,
near his aunts and uncles—
not in Georgia with three generations of her family.
They decide to hold a memorial service
for him a few days later in Atlanta.

The crowd outside the stairwell grows,
keeps vigil for a dozen hours—
they tell stories, make calls, write an obituary,
organize airplane tickets to Connecticut
for twenty people and a casket.
She and their children hold his hands and feet,
talk to him as, near midnight, he slips away.

~

In the softly-lit room with silk flowers
someone comes to tell her that his organs
are too compromised to be donated.

A nun brings her his wallet,
his glasses, his wedding ring.

He Taught Them How to Shovel

He taught our children
how to lift Georgia red clay
with the face of a shovel—
the bend of knees,
the crook of elbows,
the turn of shoulders,
the twist of wrists—
the rhythm of a job well done.

~

Twilight near midnight
his heart is at the end—
our children and I
hold his hands,
fingers, toes,
talk to him,
talk to one another across his body—
to ease his travel
to ease our last kisses.

~

The polished walnut box
is lowered, hands release ropes;
it catches half way down
then settles at the bottom.
Rabbi Tam spills the first earth
onto the coffin,
hands me the shovel.
I spill earth onto the box,
hand the shovel to our children.
They borrow a five dollar bill
from Uncle Lenny,
drop it into the grave,

Travelin' money, Dad.
You always made sure we had travelin' money.

~

Our son and daughters shovel
the frozen Connecticut earth—
earth on wood,
earth on earth,
until they have buried their father.

4400 Loblolly Trail

For Howard, my husband

1.

Home. Cedar house on an oak-covered hill,
golden siding under the east eaves,
on the west splintering, silvering.
Howard took a year off to build this house—
supervised by our three-year-old son,
self-anointed *Joshua King of the Mountain*
standing atop a mound of red Georgia dirt
his father had pulled to shape the foundation.
Nail guns and skill saws, levels and ladders.
Howard framed the walls, hired a few men
to help raise them and to sling the trusses into place,
leaving space for two west-facing kitchen skylights.
Hearths of brick my grandfather had salvaged
from the nineteenth-century Atlanta City Hall.

Under the front stairwell, a cubby—
bare light bulb and faux paneling;
our children kitted it out with cushions and crayons,
books, boxed drinks, scissors and tape,
Elmer's glue, a purloined stapler,
and a menagerie of stuffed animals.
In this cubby, Joshua cut a patch of his sister
Rebecca's cascading curls right down
to her three-year-old scalp.

Judith, our youngest, announced to anyone who'd listen,
I got the last pair of blue eyes in Mommy's tummy.
Red-headed woodpeckers breakfasted
on the master bedroom chimney—
perfectly pitched for reveille.
Wrens swooped down the living room chimney,
nested in a sterling pitcher—
fledglings learned to fly inside the house.

Big Wheels ripped down the hill,
up a wheelchair ramp built for my mother,
screeching in a halt of black tracks on the deck.
Mice *taste-tested* Rebecca's scratch pound cake
the night before final competition at the county fair.
Rabbits—Thor, Snookums, and Oreo.
Generations of dogs—Argo, Wilberforce, Squash,
Tuxedo, Mr. Enormous, Agatha, Puppy,
Romulus and Remus, Pyramus, and Thisbee.

Black steel circular staircase
to the children's bedrooms—
a percussion instrument for spoons and sticks
and children's pissed-off stomping feet.
Clandestine magazines under Joshua's bed.
The door between Rebecca's and Judith's rooms
slamming and slamming, shaking the house.
Howard sealing it shut with tenpenny nails.
Sheetrock walls in the girls' bathroom
—an ever-expanding mural under Judith's direction—
flowers and trees, faces, sailboats,
random names and words, quotes and poems,
a reminder over the toilet to boys to put the seat down.
Stashed under the sink: brushes and half-pints
of Home Depot paint alongside tampons and towels.

In the kitchen— a fireplace, a fifty gallon fish tank,
a hamster habitrail and a black six burner commercial stove.
Dad's cooking lesson—*Throw spaghetti
at the kitchen ceiling. If it sticks, it's done.*
One Valentine's Day we surprised our children
with fifty homemade valentines hanging
from the ten-foot kitchen ceiling—
large and small ones, red, white and pink
construction paper with glitter, ribbons and paper lace.

In the dining room—a sixteen-foot table
Howard built of heart-cut pine—the setting for

matchbox car races, solar system construction,
black-tie dinners, curtain sewing, backgammon games,
southern breakfasts for out-of-town guests—
fried chicken, ham, grits, biscuits, scrambled eggs,
fresh squeezed orange juice and hot coffee.

One night lightning screamed the length
of a giant loblolly pine at the foot of the driveway,
jumped the metal *No Trespassing* sign,
kicked up two feet of dirt as it hit the ground.

2.

Howard and I are married
twenty-seven and a half years.
He dies of a heart attack
in the cardiac care unit
of St. Joseph's Hospital.

I wake the next morning
in a half-empty king-sized bed.

4400 Loblolly Trail overflows
with sobs, with the stories and laughter
of family and friends from as far away as Alaska,
with food and drink— *kugel* and brisket,
chicken and dumplings, homemade brownies.
I have no idea who brings the food,
boxes of Kleenex, bottles of *schnapps*,
who keeps the kitchen clean,
takes out the garbage, feeds the dogs,
who answers the telephone.

We *sit shiva* for seven days—
a brief service each evening
around the table that Howard built,
led by men who'd known him well
and one evening by two teenaged sisters
who called him *Uncle Howard.*

We mumble the ancient mourner's prayer,
Y is-ga-dal v'yis-ka-dash sh'may ra-bo....

On the eighth evening
Joshua, Rebecca, Judith and I welcome quiet—
stillness within the walls of the cedar house
their father had hammered into a home.
    Crescent moon slips across the kitchen skylights.

Jumping off the Refrigerator

For our children—Joshua, Rebecca, and Judith

I miss you jumping off the top of the refrigerator,
one by one into your father's arms, giggling the whole way

and the *latkes* Dad made by the dozens
we took to your elementary school classes during Chanukah.

I miss the rust-red door from the kitchen pantry
into the dining room, kitchen walls yellow, then blue.

I miss the song of the sump pump in the lowest corner of the basement
and field-mice droppings in pots and pans under the kitchen sink in winter.

I miss Dad lining up a gaggle of little girls horizontally
across the sixteen-foot dining room table he built,
pretending to be the lion trainer Gunther Gabel-Williams,
and directing the girls to roll over as one, rise up on their knees and roar.

I miss Joshua throwing up all over the kitchen floor
in the middle of his eleventh birthday party.

I miss Dad spending hours at the kitchen table
helping Judith organize her math notebook

and Rebecca swimming year-round—her collection
of chlorine-shredded bathing suits on the bathroom floor.

I miss Oreo, the flop-eared rabbit who burrowed
into Joshua's box springs to hide, and Snookums
the white rabbit with pink eyes and a huge goiter,
which no doubt accounted for his ill temper.

I miss the afternoon Dad flipped the antique kitchen table,
dishes flying everywhere—frustrated dealing with
multiple generations of my family, their lawyers
and accountants as we went about selling the family farm

and the three of you, terrified,
running out of the kitchen to hide in a huddle.

I miss celebrations at home—dancing the *hora* into the yard
during your Bat and Bar Mitzvah parties,
and the black-tie twenty-fifth anniversary party
you organized with a stack of hundred dollar bills Dad gave to you.

I miss his closet of blue Brooks Brothers boxer shorts,
well-worn overalls and tuxedos and his hat collection—
from a Sherlock Holmes deerstalker to a black beaver-top hat.

I miss Dad's bedtime stories of the Tweedie-Dum-Dinkums—
how he'd sometimes fall asleep in your beds before you did.

I miss standing in your bedrooms after each of you left for college—
mismatched sneakers, papers and notebooks askew,
abandoned clothes, soccer and swimming trophies,
your odor on the pillows.

I miss the sand pile and rusting Tonka toys
—some from your childhood, some from mine—
        morning sunshine in the nursery.

She — Part Two

She is less afraid than she used to be,
walks fifty yards in the dark
from the carport to the kitchen door—
dried leaves rustle in the woods,
night shadows sway,
a tiny screech owl shrieks its bone-chilling call.
She is fifty-three, has been a widow for six months,
her children at colleges and universities
in Massachusetts, Ohio, and Connecticut.

She has bought a cell phone,
had an alarm system installed in the house.
She shops for one person at the grocery store—
two apples, six eggs, half a pound of deli turkey.
She wraps and freezes single servings
of steak and chicken breasts,
pumps gas into her eight-year-old
dark blue Honda Accord—no one else to do it.

She sits on the edge of what was once *their* bed,
her body wracked with the shakes, but she cannot cry.
A kudzu of dirty bras, panties, and jeans
breeds on door knobs and the bathroom floor;
unmade bed sheets gather dust and dog hair,
fatigued eyes stare at her from the morning mirror,
three days' worth of dirty dishes scattered
from room to room, lunches of nachos,
Coca-Cola, chocolate discs on rosemary bread.
A psychologist advises her to go to yoga classes
twice a week. She believes yoga is for the young and lithe,
doesn't know one end of a yoga mat from another.
A young flautist, who'd composed music
for her husband's memorial service,
takes her the first few times. She keeps going.

Two years pass. She sells her house,
the one her husband built—home of safety and silliness,
home of *If you don't pick up all the toys and clothes,*
they're going into a garbage bag and disappear,
home of a basketball hoop over the mudroom door,
a Trash 80 computer and unfolded laundry,
home of college acceptances and rejections,
elections won and lost, puppies born and old dogs buried,
home of finding her mother-in-law dead
across the bed in the guest room,
home of anger and heartbreak each time
she smelled cigarettes on her husband's breath,
home of watching the Muppets as a family every Saturday night,
home of *sitting shiva* for the father of her children,
the man she loved who loved her without reserve.

~

She builds a new house on her land
along the Chattahoochee River—
a smaller home, mostly one floor,
grab-bars in the master shower for when she grows old,
an attached garage that opens into the mud room,
lots of glass—windows, doors, and skylights
to bring the outdoors inside, even in winter.
She brings to the new house five generations of family photos,
the sixteen foot slab-table her husband built of heart-cut pine,
and a clear glass flask of *white lightnin'* cooked in the woods
by childhood neighbor Mr. Duncan, who floated his merchandise
down one creek into the river and out a creek on the other side
to avoid the revenuers.

She goes to yoga class twice a week,
has replaced the blue Honda with a red Saab 9-5
but never drives above the speed limit,
still believing from her teen years that cops
stop red cars for speeding more often than others.
She's completed a study for a corporate foundation

on the religious right's impact on public education,
celebrated her children's high school,
college, and graduate school graduations,
danced on a California ranch at her son's wedding,
flown to London to hold her first grandchild.

~

A widow for eight years. She looks away and aches
when she passes older couples holding hands
or sharing meals in restaurants, but is embarrassed at the idea
of being seen in public with a man not her late husband.
She tries internet dating—has a breakfast date with
a Jewish veterinarian whose hands tremble
as he cuts his pancakes cross-ways from all directions
before slathering the plate with syrup. Her life-long friend
forgets to call her with an excuse to get away.
She accepts an invitation from other friends for supper
and *Othello* at the Shakespeare Tavern in downtown Atlanta,
arrives to find a tall man with gray curly hair sitting alone
eating a salad at their reserved table. She thinks,
How rude of him not to wait, but lets that go and joins him
stifling laughter at the eye-level Dr. Scholl's inserts
in Othello's sandals.

The man with grey curls is an artist;
she visits his downtown studio.
He comes to her house for an afternoon walk by the river,
looks at a snapshot of her late husband and says,
He must have laughed a lot.
He stays so long she invites him for supper,
defrosts one small steak, one piece of salmon—
all there is in her freezer.

He comes back often; she buys larger steaks,
double-checks herself in the mirror—
often changing outfits more than once.
They laugh through a summer rich

with friends, lamb with garlic, roasted eggplant,
a Hugh Masekela concert, walks through the woods,
an exhibition of postcards of lynchings.
He plays Leonard Cohen CDs—
Dance me through the panic 'til I'm safely gathered in
but he cannot dance her around the kitchen.

She begins to write poetry—in the mornings in her head
while walking by the river, on the computer while eating lunch,
on folded-in-half sheets of paper she keeps in her purse
while waiting for the dentist or an airplane,
on a yellow pad bedside her bed at two in the morning—
not the rhyming doggerel quatrains
she'd once composed for birthdays or anniversaries,
but deluges of stanzas about him, about her,
about them, about *what-the-hell-is-happening-here?*
She decides to show him some of her poems—
words on the page that say things she cannot say out loud.
He tells her, *Your poems are good;*
you have to take your writing seriously,
makes her stand in the living room,
introduce herself to an invisible audience,
read her poems aloud.
She gets the giggles like a schoolgirl,
is afraid to tell her children about him.

Three months after Othello-and-the-Dr.-Scholl's-inserts,
summer days begin to shorten. He closes his studio
in Atlanta, packs his canvases and brushes,
his easels and paint-splattered shoes, packs the shadows
of his brawls with depression, his collapsed relationships,
packs it all into his gray Dodge Ram truck
with a camper-top on the back and prepares to move
to Vermont to house-sit his sister's lake house
through the fall and winter—
no idea if he'll ever return to Georgia.
Over a final shared meal in her kitchen,
he hands her a sketch of a woman dozing on a sofa.

He has written on the back—
Waking up—from a long rest!

Full-throated tree frogs
escort his gray truck out the gravel drive.
She sinks slowly to the ground.
Tail lights fade in the dusk.
She walks through the house turning on lights,
setting the alarm.

~

She registers for her first poetry workshop—
a week in the north Georgia mountains.
She locks her house, climbs into her red Saab
feeling more vulnerable than she's ever felt
as she drives alone for two hours to the workshop.
She begins to write poems that are not about the artist—
but the change of seasons, the farm where she grew up,
the meadow by the Chattahoochee river
where she and her dogs walk each morning,
her husband's burial, her politics,
her father's distortions, her mother's hands.
Back in Atlanta she is invited to join
a weekly workshop of experienced poets, a master class.
She is intimidated, hardly opens her mouth
for the first few weeks.

~

Nine months after the artist left for Vermont,
he drives back south to Georgia, straight to her house.
In the back of his gray Dodge truck is a new series called
Metamorphosis—seven large paintings of butterflies
with their caterpillars and chrysalises—
blue morph, cloudless sulphur, monarch, orange Nero.
He settles his studio and klediments
into a once-lovely-now-run-down old house

half an hour away on Juniper Street in mid-town Atlanta.

She cuts red camellia blossoms and cotoneaster berries,
dusty pink hellebores and orange quince branches,
puts them in her grandmother's Rookwood vases.
She checks her hair and make-up, holds in her stomach,
renews her two-seat theatre subscription.
He urges her to attend weeklong poetry workshops
in the California San Jacinto mountains
and in Paris, not far from her grandchild in London.
He house-sits her dogs, begins a series of paintings
of women, men, and families impacted by breast cancer,
invites her to interview the twenty-one models
and write their stories. She hems and haws for a week.
I haven't had breast cancer. How can I do justice to the models?
I'm trying to finish my first book of poetry.
He suggests he'll ask someone else—she says *Yes.*

Red Clay, a chapbook of her poetry is published;
she participates in poetry readings with less stammer,
dares to call herself *a poet.* Beside her house,
he builds a garden shed with a roof of blooms—
sunflowers, daisies, yellow and red million bells,
cascades of morning glories and woodbine.
She lets her hair grow out gray.
He gives talks on art and ethics at Emory University,
turns on Pablo Casals's Bach *Suites.*
They host dinner parties—whole red snapper
stuffed with asparagus and pearl onions,
rock Cornish game hens in an apricot glaze.
He moves his studio into a barn across
the creek and granite outcropping from her house—
the barn her husband built after most of the family farm
was sold to a developer—tractors, a bush hog, road scraper,
three generations of metal- and wood-working tools,
compressors that work and don't work, saddles and bridles,
a lobster trap, sleigh bells, carapace of a sea turtle.
Her children in New York, New Jersey, and California

are offended/angry/hurt that he is settling into *Dad's barn*—
It is the only place left that was mostly Dad's,
a place we could just hang out with him.

She sits on her front steps and sobs—
sobs on and off for weeks,
says to her children,
It's been nearly ten years since Dad died.
The barn is not a museum. Others have had keys,
used or borrowed the tools, built things there.
It's all yours. Come and take
whatever you want or are worried about.
But they don't.

      ~

The artist changes his address to hers,
plants a vegetable garden—green beans and peas,
carrots, romaine lettuce, Japanese eggplant,
cayenne peppers, three kinds of tomatoes.
She plants basil and sage, parsley, thyme,
rosemary and two kinds of oregano.
He bush-hogs the meadow by the river,
pulls the ditches and scrapes the gravel roads.
Together they publish *A Celebration of Healing*—
an art book, a book of stories—his breast cancer paintings
and her narratives of the twenty-one models.
They carry Pyramus, an ailing fourteen-year-old
mixed-breed dog, to the vet, stay with him
as he is put to sleep. The artist buries him in the woods,
covers the grave with plywood and concrete blocks
to keep coyotes from digging it up—to no avail.

She fills summer pots with geraniums and impatiens,
ferns and sedum, tiny little daisies, begonias and heliotrope.
Their children and grandchildren come to visit;
they adopt Jimmy, a Humane Society puppy;
nurse one another through a shoulder replacement,

an intestine resection, meniscus and cataract surgeries.
They compost. They unhobble shadows of his history and of hers.
He plants an apple and a peach tree, climbing roses.
She makes arugula and avocado salad—
extra virgin olive oil and fresh lemon juice dressing.
He cooks risotto with wild mushrooms—
chanterelles, oysters, and shiitakes,
He opens a bottle of Central Coast pinot,
turns on Chopin's *Preludes*.
She sets the table with yellow placemats,
sienna Seagrove pottery candlesticks,
Himalayan salt, a red pepper grinder.
She picks King Alfreds and Narcissus poeticus

> *drops them into the turquoise urn–shaped Pisgah vase*
> *my mother used for daffodils.*

III

~ in the church he came to for refuge ~

Arabia Mountain, DeKalb County, Georgia

For Sal

Yesterday you and I climbed Arabia Mountain—
four-million-year old granite monadnock,
fifty to one hundred million years older than
its more celebrated neighbor Stone Mountain—
once owned by the Venable brothers who burned
crosses on its summit during my childhood.
The state of Georgia purchased Stone Mountain in 1958,
installed a cable car to the top,
railroad around the bottom, riverboat on the lake,
and now summer laser shows light up
Confederate heroes carved into the mountainside.

We climbed Arabia Mountain,
part of a nature reserve given to DeKalb County
in the 1970s by the Davidson family—
climbed cautiously, not to favor
our sixty-year-old knees but to avoid
oases of hundred-year-old mosses and lichen
in dozens of shades of green and burnt red—
endangered amphianthus, bright red diamorpha,
black-spored quillwort. A lone pine tree,
impudent blue and yellow wildflowers
poke through cracks in the barren rock.

You looked behind, waiting for me,
lines on your face disappearing
in the wash of an unbroken breeze,
your chambray blue shirt and white curls against
the naked stone and tranquil spring clouds.

Returning to Arabia's base we startled
a twelve-point white-tailed buck
camouflaged in the brush and trees,
crossed a two-lane road to explore

the abandoned Davidson quarry,
part of the same geologic seam as the mountain—
thousands upon thousands of Tidal Grey granite shards
stamp-size to twenty-foot slabs polished *in situ*.
A wild turkey with a near-silent guttural call
herded her seventeen chicks to safety
in the overgrown ruins of a work shack,
a frog ribbited beside a pool of rainwater,
a spring peeper let you stroke the back of its head.

Arabia Mountain would not be welcoming
in summer's heat nor winter's ice,
but yesterday, the rains of early May just past,
you looked especially handsome.

The Church – 1988

Pantoum for Sal's brother John, 1952-1988

He came to the church for solace
the church of his parents, three brothers, and a sister
the church of Bach solos he sang as a boy
the choir loft always his sanctuary

in the church of his parents, three brothers, a sister
the church with two organs and eight thousand pipes
the choir loft always his sanctuary
organ swells wrapping around him

from the eight thousand pipes in the church
where, as a child, perfect pitch was his hallmark
organ swells wrapping around him
in the church where, at thirty-six, he came seeking peace

perfect pitch as a tenor still his hallmark in the choir
sixteenth-century tapestries softening the songs
in the church where he came seeking peace
the church with a sun-lit rose window

sixteenth century tapestries softening the songs
in the church where he came to for refuge
the church with a sun-lit rose window
the church that was founded by abolitionists

the church where he came to for refuge
AIDS tracing his body, racing through lymph glands
as he walked into the church of abolitionists
with a sore on his back that wouldn't heal

AIDS tracing his body, racing through lymph glands
pneumonia his constant companion
a sore on his that back wouldn't heal
his breath giving out as he climbed up the stairs

pneumonia his constant companion
mind muddled with dementia
his breath giving out as he climbed up the stairs
his design studio in a shambles

mind muddled with dementia
believing the hot water faucet ran cold water
his design studio in a shambles
his guitar untouched in its case

believing the hot water faucet ran cold water
harmonic triads no equal for the nightmares
his guitar unplayed in its case
his quick wit overcome by the terrors

harmonic triads no equal for the nightmares
Would family and friends now abandon him?
his quick wit overcome by the terrors
seventeen thousand for drugs every month

Would family and friends now abandon him?
no health insurance to be had in his name
seventeen thousand for drugs every month
and a nurse told him what *she* would do,

if no health insurance to be had in her name
she'd get hold of a gun and end it all quickly
the nurse told him that's what she'd do
so John came to the church for comfort

pondering if he should end it all quickly
and the minister counseled him
in the church where he'd come to for comfort
You are gay. I cannot help you

the minister counseled him
This is God's revenge.

You are gay. I cannot help you still ringing in his ears
alone in his apartment two weeks later

in his head *This is God's revenge*
in his hands a gun purchased at a flea market
alone in his apartment two weeks later
no one knows who'd taught John how to use it

the handgun he'd bought at a flea market
how to use it without leaving too gruesome a mess
no one knows who had taught him
to hold it at the side of his jaw pointing up

so as not to leave too gruesome a mess
John came to the church in a wooden coffin
the gun at the side of his jaw'd done its work
the church brimming with flowers

when John came to the church in a wooden coffin
Ruby from the dry cleaners sobbing
in the church brimming with flowers
the local bank president slipping into a pew

Ruby from the dry cleaners sobbing
in the barrel-vaulted nearly-filled church
the local bank president slipping into a pew
gay friends uncertain about where they should sit

in the barrel-vaulted nearly-filled church
the minister who'd shunned John leading the service
gay friends uncertain about where they should sit
the minister inviting no eulogies

the minister who'd shunned John leading the service
in the church of Bach solos John sang as a boy
in the church where the minister invited no eulogies
in the church John had come to for solace

The Winds

One might not know the winds
had come brutal
thundering down hard across the hill
but for the trunk
of a seventy-five year old hickory twisted off
three feet from the ground
roots freed in a great burst of red-orange earth
long limbs heavy with clusters
of a thousand hard black nuts slamming
across the creek, damning the water
a pulverized loblolly
releasing its odor of pine resin,
its bruises tracing the bark
of a sixty-foot oak
bullied to the earth by the hickory.

~

In this musky-sweet,
suddenly-silent place,
young bucks scratch the velvet itch
of fledgling racks
on newly reachable limbs.

The Church – 2000

Southern Baptist Church near Newnan, Georgia

White clapboard church, modest steeple,
flat-trimmed bushes either side of the front steps.
Brown upright piano behind and to the right
of the preacher's pedestal. The church pianist

softly playing *Blessed Assurance.*
Folks taking their seats
for thirty-five year old Sam's funeral.
Sam's partner of ten years, having been

excluded from *family prayers* in the preacher's study,
slips into a wooden pew near the back of the church—
white wadded-up handkerchief twisted in his hands.
Gay and straight friends surround him.

The service lasts less than half an hour.
The preacher, a thin man in a black suit,
white shirt and black tie, only makes
eye contact with *family* in the first few rows.

His homily: *People stray and make mistakes.*
This is God's revenge. Sam's partner is not invited
to eulogize Sam—as if such exclusions
make him invisible sobbing in the hall.

The Firewood Pile

Bless the firewood pile dwindling down
to a single horizontal row bermed
with pine needles, winter leaves of oak and beech—
browns and silvers, highlights of amber.

Bless the last log stacked on the pile in summer,
first off at early frost,
leaving untouched the bottom row
now unto four years.

Bless the oak logs sponged with time and rain
melting into one another,
chunks calving against the grain,
soft splinters, veins of mildew.

Bless ants and mites in their enterprise
and a blue-tailed skink resting in the sun,
and spiders, maybe a black widow with its red hourglass,
perhaps a snake, a green garter, please not a copperhead.

Bless our dog Joe in his tireless efforts to reorder
the firewood, carrying it piece by piece across the yard,
Bless each feathery limb of the hemlock
standing guard over the logs.

Bless the great blue heron sentinel on the Chattahoochee shoals
turning its long neck to look at me. Bless the osprey
patrolling the river for a breakfast of rainbow trout
and bless the cluster of golden finches chattering in our garden.

IV

~ terraced the hills, purchased dairy cows ~

Cow Paths

Cow path: the creation of the cows themselves, who, having created it, follow
it or depart from it according to their whims or their needs. From daily use,
the path undergoes change. A cow is under no obligation to stay.
                                    —E. B. White

~cow path: the creation of the cows themselves~
In the 1930s along a mile of the Chattahoochee River
in the Pinkneyville Militia District of Georgia,
my grandfather, Frank Neely, bought four hundred acres
of eroded red hills, dirt roads, barren bottomlands,
of virgin loblolly pines, white and red oaks, hickories, and maples,
of natural draws carrying rainwater downhill to creeks and the river.
He developed the land in *a scientific manner* seeking
advice from the University of Georgia Ag School—
terraced the hills, bought cows that naturally fertilized the pastures
leaving cow paths crisscrossing to trees for summer shade,
to salt licks and water, to gates opening twice a day at milking time.
Crops were rotated in order to improve soil structure and fertility,
soybeans were planted and plowed under to fix nitrogen in the soil,
water was pumped from the river to irrigate fields,
blue Ford and red International Harvester tractors pulled
plows and harrows, seeders, bush-hogs, hay bailers.
The gale machine cut and blew corn through its
brontosaurus-like neck into wagons headed back to fill
two silver metal silos and one red wooden one.
Rent was paid *in-kind* for moonshining deep in the woods.

~who, having created it, follow it~
The farm was my grandparents' weekend retreat.
Their house, referred to as the Big House,
(though only one story and not particularly big)
was built of bricks salvaged from the original Atlanta City Hall,
floor to ceiling west windows faced down across
pastures and bottomlands all the way to the river.
My grandmother poured over vegetable and flower catalogs
from Wayside and Burpee, designed gardens

of peonies, gardenias and camellias, climbing roses,
of winding borders of pansies and tulips,
great swaths of bearded iris and daffodils,
pear trees espaliered against the south-facing wall of the house,
rows of mimosa trees outlining the circular front driveway.

My grandfather never stopped studying ways
to improve the land and the production of the dairy herd—
at one point cross-breeding Guernseys and Holsteins
to improve the quantity and butterfat content of the milk.
To my grandmother's chagrin, he regularly invited
civic colleagues, community leaders and business associates
to come out for weekend meetings. At the Big House
they entertained newspaper editors and college presidents,
garden clubs, the Federal Reserve Southeastern Board,
Georgia governors and, one day, Eleanor Roosevelt.

~or depart from it according to their whims or their needs~
My brothers and I grew up on the Neely Farm
in a two-story white clapboard house spared
during the Civil War by General Sherman's troops
who had camped across the river, stolen chickens
and hams from the barn until the women,
(left behind while the men and boys went off to war),
leveled buckshot at them.
We knew the steady rhythm of a paddle churning buttermilk,
the odor of windrows of alfalfa hay drying in summer heat,
the recoil and echo of shotguns during fall dove hunts,
(when the phone and electric lines were hit as often as the birds).
We left our footprints beside those of raccoons
in the soft sand of dirt roads. We saddled and bridled horses,
cantered past pigpens and four-board fence bull enclosures,
past creosote-green milking barns, calf sheds, silos,
past machine repair workshops and filled haylofts,
past the house of Mr. Ramey, the head dairyman,
and the houses of farm-worker families—Bobbie Lee and
Neal McClendon, Willie Carrol and Artee Moore,
past Miss Lizzie's house, fat beefsteak tomatoes in her garden,

sweet potatoes pies cooling on her windowsill.
We'd go to the Big House for Sunday lunch—
farm raised chicken, beets, okra, wild asparagus,
sweet corn ten minutes from stalk to table.

~from daily use, the path undergoes change~
My husband Howard and I married
under a centenarian oak in the backyard
of the white clapboard house the Yankees didn't burn;
returned to San Francisco where we'd met for three years,
then sold our bed, dining room table and chairs,
packed the rest into an orange U-Haul and drove
with our Newfoundland puppy across the country
to a cottage on the dairy farm where I grew up,
built a house on a forested hill and, in turn,
brought each of three newborn children home to the farm—
Judith, Joshua and Rebecca who stubbed their toes
on this Georgia earth, swam in the pond and river,
splashed up and down the creek, raced and slid
through rows of corn in the *irrigation rain.*
Newborn calves suckled their small hands and fingers.

Rebecca always insisted on riding the tallest horse
even if she could hardly sit astride the wide saddle;
Joshua would stand between his father's knees,
wrap his small fingers around the steering wheel
of Big Blue, the Ford *8000* tractor, and proudly *drive* it;
Judith, at seven, ran away farther than usual one afternoon,
leaving her red Snoopy suitcase behind an oak tree in the yard,
terrifying us as evening crept in and neighbors came
to help search until Remus, the dog that followed her
everywhere, began to bark, signaling their hiding place
in a decrepit shed in the woods. (Years later
we learned a snake had kept them company.)

Howard organized snipe hunts, took children for hayrides
at the annual Pinkneyville Spring Festival;
he fought Gwinnett County to keep the farm taxed

as the working dairy farm it was,
(not as *highest potential use* which the law allowed).
He was labeled a *communist* for his lobbying efforts
to protect the Chattahoochee River from developers
as they bought up river front property, bulldozed
to the water's edge, threatening flood plains
and underground aquifers with with multi-story buildings
and acres of concrete parking lots.

—a cow is under no obligation to stay—
We were the last of the family on the land.
Rebecca, Judith, and Joshua walked to the barns
to catch the school bus—cutting a wide path
as they passed *Food*, a steer being fattened for butchering.
My brothers settled with their families in other states.
My mother survived into her early eighties—
her last thirteen years disabled, living in an apartment,
needing round-the-clock care; her house rented
to a young family, descendants of the family
whose ancestors shot buckshot at the Yankees.
My grandparents lived into their nineties
spending final years in the Big House—
Miss Lizzie preparing their meals, keeping a slightly
suspicious eye on the nurses taking care of them.

Howard kept a modest peace in the family
as the decision was made to sell the farm.
Buyers came and went over the months until
a deal was done and yellow bulldozers gnashed
wide swaths across fields and through the woods.
Strangers moved into the Neely Farm subdivision—
five and six bedroom houses with three or four chimneys.
Howard reached out to welcome the *farmers,*
as they called themselves, helped with an annual pig roast,
drove the tractor and hayride for neighborhood festivities.
I was less willing to engage, feeling we'd sold the land,
which was hard enough, but not the family name.
He died ten years after the sale of the farm.

Two years later, I sold our home and a few acres of land—
which, in turn, was re-sold to another developer who bulldozed
the house to make room for a *reserve* of exclusive houses.

~I build a new home on land I had kept, down a gravel road,~
close to the river. My children, (by now I refer to them
as *my* children, feeling a bit guilty no longer saying *our* children),
visit from London, New York, and Chicago.
This is not the place we grew up—
farm fields and pastures surveyed into three hundred
lockstep lawns, no wild onions or clover in these yards,
no ditches filled with blue cornflowers and purple vetch.
The draws flood with storm-sewer water,
carrying flotsam and jetsam of neon yellow tennis balls,
red plastic cups and empty Heineken cans downstream.
Fly-fisherman in Orvis waders stand
on the Chattahoochee shoals and pee,
middle-aged men in red and green kayaks slip from the river
into the creek for Saturday morning marijuana,
inflatable Santa Clauses and lighted wire deer nod
as whitetail doe and buck cross the asphalt
foraging for winter pansies.

Vapor streetlights numb night skies,
no barns, no silos, no perfume of milk and manure,
no apple trees, no blackberry brambles,
no bulls breaking down four-board fences at night,
no pump houses to heat in winter,
no screech of disc plows being sharpened, sparks flying,
no dawn-song of a dairyman calling cows to milking,
no cow paths crisscrossing fertile pastures,
no evening calls of whip-poor-wills,
no North Star visible
as I turn onto the gravel road for home.

Requiem

The woodland hills have been stripped
of hundred-year-old white and red oaks,
of dogwoods with trunks ten inches in diameter,
a beech tree carved half a century ago
with initials inside a lopsided heart,
and a grass-skirted dancer in a bra top.

Bulldozer blades rip through the understory
of redbuds and maples, native azaleas;
twelve and fourteen foot-thick roots jerked
from the earth rest on their sides,
tentacles jutting in all directions;
mazes of Caterpillar tracks crisscross the naked hill.

The woodland hills have been stripped
of moss and a dozen kinds of ferns,
of wild mushrooms and rabbit warrens,
of buckeye and wild rose briars,
of spring carpets of mayapple and trillium,
of night paths of the shy sandy fox,

canopy nests of brazen squirrels,
and of the bounty of acorns whitetail deer await,
dust filling their nostrils—disoriented as am I,
who for decades inhaled the seasons here
where red-tailed hawk fledglings
learned to ride the thermals above
virgin hickory and loblolly pines,

and one fall afternoon I glimpsed
a golden eagle vanishing into the gloaming.

The Sycamores Weep

1.

Early mornings I walk the meadow
where wild grasses go to seed
and Buck Creek meets the Chattahoochee River,
where Jimmy and Joe, my brown and white
Humane Society dogs, run at mach speed
to herd congregations of red-breasted robins
pecking at the dirt for spring grubs and worms,
where barred owls call from deep in the woods
who cooks for you, who cooks for you,
where great horned owlets fledge
and the trumpet and rattling chorus
of migrating sandhill cranes reverberates,
where summer thunderheads pile one on top of another
and sixty-foot sycamores drop their bark
leaving sheets of silver footprints.

2.

I walk the meadow of silver footprints,
purple spiderwort and white daisy fleabane,
volunteer violets and daffodils in April,
twelve-point buck in rut lock antlers pushing
one another toward the creek, claiming mating rights;
a pair of coyotes sprinting up out of the creek hell-bent
for Jimmy—just four months old, not twenty yards from me—
Joe aggressively chasing them back across the creek,
tripping me on his way, my glasses flying, knees skinned.
I walk the meadow of remains of coyote night kills—
sinew and bone of a deer haunch, a shiny blue-black heap
of intestines, a shredded stomach spilling undigested acorns;
the meadow of a dozen bloodied black, white and red feathers
scattered among meaty joints of Pileated woodpecker bones.

3.

I walk the meadow of Pileated feathers,
where four generations of my family have watched

73

the Perseid meteor showers, squinted into the night sky
finding Ursa Major and Pegasus, the meadow
of toddlers running, falling, giggling, puppies romping,
where boys have *driven* Big Blue, the Ford 8000 tractor,
as soon as they are tall enough to stand and hold
the steering wheel, where teenaged girls have practiced
parallel parking in the red 1985 Ford pick-up,
where I danced the *hora* under a tent at my daughter's wedding,
where wooly sheep and men with beards float past in June clouds.
I walk the meadow of summer humming of bees and cicadas,
dogwood blossoms like snowflakes pausing before reaching
the ground, the meadow of ragweed sneezes,
lunar eclipses, and first kisses.

4.

I walk the meadow of lunar eclipses and first kisses,
mysterious dark-green grass fairy rings ten feet in diameter,
a five-hundred-year flood leaving mud seven feet up on tree trunks,
the meadow where I saw a wake of twenty vultures
motionless in a tree four days after I became a widow,
the meadow of an eight-foot concrete-block grill,
a wobbly wooden table bearing thirty-five years of knife scores
left from slicing Georgia tomatoes and Vidalia onions,
chopping chickens and baby-back ribs
as two and three generations of family and friends
come together on July fourth—hayrides and tug-o-war,
corn-shucking and softball, sparklers and s'mores, fireworks;
a Holocaust survivor singing *God Bless America* in the gloaming.

5.

In this meadow of *God Bless America* in the gloaming,
of purple redbuds and orange trumpet vines,
vandals have ripped down the *No Trespassing* signs,
tossed the eight-foot, mesh-steel grill top and
the wobbly eight-by-four-foot table into the river.
In this meadow of extended bluebird families,
of Venus and Cassiopeia, trespassers have pitched tents,
left their flotsam and jetsam—an empty suitcase one day,

74

a raft another, a pair of dirty socks, a bench
with initials carved into its weather-beaten slats.
Strangers have built campfires, left logs smoldering,
smoke curling up from the char in this meadow
of frost-jeweled spider-web doilies in the grass.

6.

February morning of frost jeweled spider-webs in the grass,
dogs race to the wooden table, foregoing their usual territorial
marking of night odors. Heads high, ears back, tails stiff.
          I look up—
the tin-roofed shed over the grill lies twisted on the ground,
ripped from its footings, its four-by-four corner posts
askew at angry angles, nails thrusting into the freezing air.
Spray-painted in black on the lumber and tin—
a circle with the letter *A* inside (an anarchist symbol),
the words *shua, boner,* and *fuck that shit,* a distorted smiley-face.
A ten-foot board is balanced at a gallows-like angle beside
five concrete blocks, one letter painted per block, *N I G G A.*
Spray painted on the tin—*nigga noose.*

7.

nigga noose painted on tin just six hundred yards downhill
from my kitchen. Scratched into the wooden table
with ball point pens, a figure holds a stick over the head
of a crouching shape, ready to strike—
the bent down shape calls out *NO MASSA,*
a stick figure hangs from a rope beside the initials *KKK;*
a few inches away a person hangs from a cross—
three tear-shaped drops fall from its right hand.
Across the table a swastika the size of my fist,
a second swastika the size of my thumb,
a rectangle labeled *God's Oven* with a knob reading
bake 4500 degrees, and inside the rectangle four stick people—
one of them crying *Help!* One a child.

8.

Four stick people, one crying *Help!* One a child.
The Chattahoochee runs hard against the shoals
where Creek and Cherokee Indians once set their weirs
and moonshiners ferried *white lightnin'*.
Two uniformed hate crimes officers, a young man and woman,
arrive, drive patrol cars off-road into the meadow,
find marijuana and bongs in the mayhem,
aerosol cans and glue for huffing.
No gang symbols. No fingerprint matches.
The mixture of hate targets, the specificity of graffiti,
the destruction and drug use suggest
white, internet-surfing, middle school kids—
kids who live nearby in five and six-bedroom houses,
kids unaware that I am Jewish.

9.

Neighbors, aware that I am Jewish,
load the twisted tin and tagged concrete blocks
into the back of the red Ford pickup truck,
haul it to a commercial dump and return with a can of gasoline
to douse and burn the wooden table and the four-by-fours.
Cracks in thin ice patches mark deer crossings.
Red-tailed hawks scream into the thermals,
a great blue heron cruises with low and slow wing beats,
teasing the dogs with its hoarse croaking call.
Flames hot on our faces. Cold-slate sky.
Frost melts to the roots of spring grass.
Sixty-foot sycamores weep into their silver footprints
where wild grasses grow and
Buck Creek meets the Chattahoochee River.

The Neely Farm Sestina

My grandfather pieced four hundred acres into the Neely Farm—
birch and beech trees, hardscrabble hills and draws of eroded red earth,
hundred-year-old oaks and rhododendron in the bend of the Chattahoochee River
where Creek and Cherokee caught fish in weirs stretched shore to shore
and moonshiners ferried liquid gold, avoiding revenuers by night.
Orion's Belt, the Big Dipper, and Venus—astronomy in night skies.

Four generations of my family galloped horses under cumulus skies,
across terraced hills and quilts of fields—a dairy farm.
Guernsey and Holstein bulls broke through fences at night,
silage corn grew twenty-five feet tall in the Georgia earth,
mazes of irrigation pipes in the bottomlands carried water
into massive rainbow arcs pumped from the river.

Only catfish before Buford Dam, no trout in the river,
white-washed fences against thunderhead skies,
garbage dumped into the Chattahoochee water,
cows flicked flies with their tails, won awards for the Neely Farm.
Five-thousand-year-old arrowheads surfaced in harrowed earth,
scent of fresh-cut timothy and alfalfa hay on summer nights.

Foxes in chicken houses, firewood for winter nights,
alluvial soil after spring floods of the river.
The *honey-wagon* with its cortege of flies replenished the earth,
calves frolicked alongside honeysuckle under sunset skies,
apples, asparagus, and blackberries grew wild on the farm.
We scrubbed our hands for supper with Ivory soap and water.

Discs on plows tightened in parallel place, wells of spring water,
tandem tractors tilled the land until gloaming became night.
Now milking barns are only memories in photographs of the Neely Farm,
no silos, no harrows turning fields by the river.
Strangers call this land *home*, asphalt streets, grey winter skies,
no arrowheads and pottery shards rising through plowed earth.

Storm sewers flood the draws, three hundred manicured lawns hide red earth,
five and six bedroom houses, swim teams in chlorined pool water,
lighted tennis courts dull constellation-less skies,
no North Star visible turning onto dirt roads for home at night,
no dawn-song of a dairyman calling cows from the river,
no perfume of milk and manure on a dairy farm.

My children stubbed their toes on this earth, swam in the river's cold water,
newborn calves suckled their fingers. Now vapor lights numb nighttime skies
and spiral topiaries frame a bronze sign with a mallard announcng Neely Farm.

V

~ hanging baskets she fills with geraniums ~

1952 Snapshot: Summer Camp, Tennessee

Five nine-year old girls in the cabin—three are Catholic
from New Orleans, one Episcopalian (Christie) from Oklahoma
and me, a Jewish girl from Georgia who's never attended
religious school. The Catholic girls sit on the floor

deep in a conversation which repeats throughout the summer—
     Who do they hate the most?
Me, because the *Jews killed Jesus and Catholicism
was the <u>first</u> religion?* Or Christie because,

How dare Episcopalians break away from the Catholic Church?
I sit silent on my top bunk, above me camper's names
and dates from the past scratched into bare wooden boards.
I don't even know enough to interrupt with,

I believe Jesus was a Jew. I can only write in large
capital letters sideways across two pages in my diary
I hate them followed by a long row of exclamation points
dug deep into the paper with my ball point pen.

1958 Snapshot: Oglethorpe 23 Bus

I am fifteen, feeling spring and pretty in a new
lavender skirt with two starched crinolines
underneath it and a matching scooped-neck blouse—
daring because my collar bones are exposed.

I'm riding the segregated Oglethorpe 23 bus
on the way to high school. A white man reeking
of liquor sits next to me, puts his left hand
on my right thigh. I get up, stand in the aisle

until my Fifth Street stop, promise myself
that if the man follows me off this bus and onto
the next one, I'll go to the back of the bus and sit
beside someone *colored* just to keep this man

　　　from sitting next to me.
　　　Even if it is against the law.

1971 Snapshot: Janice's Hanging Baskets

Janice, my neighbor, lives in the red brick
single story house at the head of the road,
sells hanging baskets she fills with geraniums,
verbena, impatiens, begonias, ferns, and mosses.

One summer morning at the door of her greenhouse,
my first-born asleep in the car a few steps away, she turns to me—
> *Eve, you're Jewish, a Biblical daughter of Sarah,*
> *who gave birth at ninety years old.*
> *Now that you are a mother you are obligated*
> *to stop the murder of unborn babies.*
> *You must become a leader in the anti-abortion movement.*

I pay for the hanging basket in my hand, go home,
water it with ice cubes like Janice taught me
so as not to flood the plants or the kitchen counter below.
The plants last through the summer,
their blossoms leaves crinkle, turn brown, and die.

1980s Snapshot: Gwinnett County
School Board Meetings

I've been elected to the Board of Education
of the fastest growing school district in the nation—
rural farms fast becoming suburban subdivisions.
Board meetings begin with everyone standing

for a prayer ending *in Je-sus name*. (In the south, pretty
much a gathering of any sort begins with a prayer to Jesus.)
I look down out of respect for others and at the same time
look around for the scout troop that will inevitably

march in with the flag for the Pledge of Allegiance.
After a few meetings I explain to the Superintendent
I feel excluded when prayers in a public governmental setting
end *in Jesus name*. Folks on the staff and Board begin to confess to me

that I am the first Jewish person they've ever met.
I take a calendar of major Jewish holidays to the Superintendent—
PTA meetings, parent conferences, exams, and sports events
are no longer scheduled on Jewish holidays. The only Rabbi
in Gwinnett County is added to a list of those invited
to offer a prayer before School Board meetings.

2009 Snapshot: Peachtree Industrial Boulevard, Chamblee, Georgia

I'm on the way to Oglethorpe Presbyterian Church
for the memorial service for my friend Eva,
born in 1929 Germany to a Christian father and
a half-Jewish mother. Eva's father divorced her mother
in 1938, in part because of *a drop of Jewish blood.*

Miraculously, Eva and her mother were never turned over
to the Nazis, survived the war eating potatoes and rutabagas.
Eva came to the University of Georgia on a Fulbright,
married a Georgia boy, lived around the world as the wife

of a foreign service officer, had two daughters and
lost a son to AIDS. I stop at a red light on Peachtree Industrial Boulevard;
a battered yellow pickup truck pulls up, eases past—
on the passenger door a magnetic American flag covers
part of the rust, in the back window hangs an empty gun rack,
on the dented bumper a bumper sticker reads:

> *I WILL FORGIVE JANE FONDA*
> *WHEN THE JEWS FORGIVE HITLER*

2015 Snapshot: Poetry Reading

I am reading *Without Sanctuary*, a poem I've written
about seeing an exhibition of one hundred and fifty
picture postcards of lynchings, to an audience
in an independent Atlanta bookstore. I recognize a few
other poets. The room is silent as I finish.

I mumble *thank you* and, on the way back to my seat,
an African American poet I know gives me a thumbs up
and a nod. I begin to breathe again. At the end
of the evening, a white man, probably near eighty,

his blue blazer loose on his shoulders, walks up to me,
shakes my hand, looks me in the eye. In a quiet, cultivated
southern voice thanks me for the poem and says,

> *I was a university frat boy during the depression.*
> *One of my friends invited me to a barbeque.* (Pause.)
>
> *I didn't understand (Long pause)*
>
> *until I got there.* (Extremely long pause. He looks down.)
>
> *It was a lynching.*

VI

~ a time when everyone knew their place ~

Without Sanctuary

Martin Luther King Center, Atlanta, Georgia, August 2002

1.

Southern trees bear strange fruit
Blood on the leaves and blood at the root

A short corridor, a scratchy recording,
Billie Holiday singing *Strange Fruit*—
her voice wrapping around me and my new friend Sal
as he and I wait our turn to enter *Without Sanctuary*—
a quiet room lit mostly with the ambient light from glass cases
filled with newspapers, flyers, pamphlets,
and nearly one hundred and fifty picture postcards of lynchings—

postcards collected by white, self-proclaimed *picker* James Allen,
who made his living buying and selling *stuff,*
who one day was proffered a picture postcard
of an African American woman hanging from a steel bridge,
a crowd of whites lined up above her to watch.

For the next twenty-five years Allen
searched for other postcards of lynchings
and the stories behind them—
scoured flea markets, estate sales,
located families of those lynched
and of those who'd attended lynchings;
unearthed faded, torn, worn-at-the-edges postcards,
mostly black-and-white or sepia, some with an *X* marking
the spot where the sender stood to watch the lynching.

2.

Scent of magnolia sweet and fresh
And the sudden smell of burning flesh

Sal and I take our place alongside silent
barely moving, stone-faced older people,

white middle-aged groups of two and three,
teenagers with hands stuck in their jean pockets,
African American parents holding children close
as they move from one postcard to the next—

Postcards of *Negroes* who'd been grabbed
(often with the collaboration of the authorities)
by *white citizen* mobs that included doctors, lawyers,
and merchants administering their own law—

Postcards of *Negroes* beaten with shovels
or whips, or castrated, or hands or ears cut off,
or bodies riddled with bullets or soaked in coal oil,
hung and set on fire—

> William Brown accused of molesting
> a white girl burns on a pyre of lumber.
> A crowd of white men in jackets, white shirts,
> and ties watch. Flames light the night darkness.
> Omaha, Nebraska, 1919

Postcards of *Negro* men stripped to the waist,
their skin racked with slash marks from beatings,
their clothes ripped to shreds, or bodies completely naked,
sometimes genitals covered with a cloth or blanket.

> W. C. Williams hangs from a tree,
> accused of murder, assaulted by a mob
> of three hundred, body riddled with bullets;
> blood streams down his legs suggesting
> he's been castrated, his lower body
> covered with a kitchen apron.
> Ruston, Louisiana, 1938

Sal and I move through the hushed exhibition alongside
an African American father in a dark suit and tie,
his wife in a red blazer and gold jewelry watching
protectively as their teenaged son and daughter

move from postcard to postcard, an elderly
African American man silent in freshly pressed overalls,
a white mother pointing at a particular postcard,
her daughter nodding—

> Augustus Goodman, alleged to have murdered
> the sheriff, dragged through town by a mob,
> hangs in broad daylight from a huge oak tree
> that serves as the community bulletin board,
> four notices nailed on its wide trunk. A dozen
> or more white men in wide brimmed hats
> turn their backs and walk away.
> Bainbridge, Georgia, 1903

3.

Pastoral scene of the gallant South
The bulging eyes and the twisted mouth

I stand still—a college-educated, southern white woman,
who, until this moment, assumed lynchings
were carried out by a handful of bigoted *rednecks*
who would take a black man deep into the woods,
string him up from a tree, leave him dead or dying.
Now I stand face to face with images of women
being lynched, of four or five *Negro* men being
simultaneously hung from the same tree,
of men hanging from bridges and rafters,
from makeshift tripod racks and streetlights, hanging
alongside public roads, in front of jails, beside courthouses—

> Charles Mitchell accused by a white widow
> of robbery and rape hangs from a tree
> in the courthouse yard, head askew
> having been jerked up and down until the crowd
> is satisfied his neck has been broken. His clothes
> and shoes collected by souvenir hunters.
> Urbana, Ohio, 1897

I had not known until this day
lynchings were celebrations,
crowds of whites could grow to ten or fifteen thousand,
including women and children dressed in Sunday best—

> *Five hundred women were in the crowd of*
> *ten thousand spectators and some helped*
> *to hang the negro and to drag the body a mile*
> *to the alleged scene of the crime.*
> New York Times, 1909

Lynching stories fueled newspaper circulation,
so newspapers published meticulous accounts—

> *Mother and son had been hauled by wagon six miles*
> *to a new steel bridge, gagged with tow sacks*
> *and hung from the bridge. The woman's arms*
> *were swinging at her side, untied, while about*
> *twenty feet away her son swung with his clothes*
> *partly torn off and his hands tied with a saddle string.*
> From Oklahoma newspapers, 1911

I had not known lynchings were commercial enterprises—
justice coupled with entertainment for which tickets
might be sold. One was held in a theatre,
a nickel bought a seat and a shot at the victim.
Lynchings were prime business for photographers
who printed and sold postcards of bodies hanging,
corpses burning, of crowds in festive spirit, souvenirs
to be mailed across the nation with careful handwriting

reporting—
> *More than twenty men were hanged*
> *upon this tree during the early days.*

bragging—
> *Well John—This is a token of a great day*
> *we had in Dallas, March 3, a negro was hung*

for an assault on a three year old girl. I saw
this on my noon hour. I was very much in the bunch.
You can see the negro hanging on a telephone pole.

or simply—
    Coon Cooking.

        4.
Here is a fruit for the crows to pluck
For the rain to gather, for the wind to suck

I whisper names of men and women
in the postcards—

        Bunk Richardson accused of rape and murder
        wears only his long johns as he hangs
        over the Coosa River, swinging next to a piling.

                    Gadsden, Alabama, 1906

        Elias Clayton, Elmer Jackson, and Isaac McGhie,
        black circus workers alleged to have assaulted
        a young white girl, dragged from the jail. Two of them
        hang just a few feet off the ground, chests bare,
        shirts pulled down to tie their hands. The third
        lies dead on the ground near their feet. A nighttime
        crowd of five thousand closes in only a yard
        or so away from the bodies.

                    Duluth, Minnesota, 1920

        Jesse Washington, a mentally retarded
        seventeen-year-old who *confessed* to murdering
        a white woman on whose farm he was a laborer.
        After a four minutes deliberation, the jury's
        guilty verdict is greeted with shouts of *Get that nigger!*
        Fifteen thousand come to the public square
        to witness Washington's hanging, climb on poles

and on top of cars, lean out of windows,
sit on one another's shoulders. Parents lift
children up for a better view as Washington
is beaten with shovels and bricks, castrated,
his ears cut off, his body lowered up and down
into a bonfire, his fingers cut off as he tries
to climb the hot chain suspending him.
His charred corpse hangs for public display
in front of a blacksmith shop. On the back
of a postcard of Washington's burned body—
   This is the barbeque we had last night.

   Waco, Texas, 1916

  5.
Black body swinging in the Southern breeze
Strange fruit hanging from the poplar trees

Outside the King Center,
Sal and I sit on a bench
near the statue of Mahatma Gandhi.
Neither of us speaks.
Others drift back outside
into the not-moving hot August air.
The only sound a police siren
going up Auburn Avenue.

Counterpoint

Something just died a prolonged and vocal death
in the woods outside my kitchen window.

Electric lights flicker, counterpoint to the dry,
gale-force north winds rattling every threshold and sash.

Hickory nuts bombard the roof;
two dogs attach themselves to my ankles
under the desk.

~

Sudden silence,
as if the gods need to catch their breath.

Limbs begin a macabre dance,
silhouettes in front of a rising moon.

Why I Am Not a Black Man

I am not a black man.
I have never been asked to pass a literacy test
in order to register to vote.
I have never been stopped by the police
because I'm driving a new car.
I have never been arrested for burglary
trying to get into my own home.
I have never been assumed to be a rap artist
I have never been called *boy*.

I am not a black man.
Nobody assumes I'm a drug dealer or a pimp.
Nobody assumes I am illiterate or unteachable.
I have never been followed by department store security,
stopped outside the door and questioned for shoplifting.
I have never been refused service at a restaurant or motel,
nor have any of my ancestors.
I have never been asked, *Do you sunburn?*

I am not a black man.
No one ever told me basketball was my *ticket out*
No one ever told me, *You people have rhythm.*
No one looks-without-looking
to see if I am unusually well hung.
I have a uterus, breasts, and my great-grandmother's
Daughters of the American Revolution certificate.

I am not a black man.
I am a white woman—though not the white
of Georgia dogwood blossoms in spring,
nor the white of starched aprons
worn over the blue and gray
maid's uniforms of my childhood.
I have never been called *the n-word*.

Daniel

1.

He was raised in a time
when everyone
knew their place—
colored and *white*,
country folk and city folk,
poor white trash and debutante,
high yaller and blue-black-skinned,
house servant and farm hand,
kids with brand-new Buster Browns,
poor kids in his all-white elementary school
whose hand-me-down shoes
were slit to make room for their toes,
a time when he practiced
the Palmer Method of cursive writing—
a No. 2 yellow pencil held gently
between his thumb and forefinger.
The only *colored* children he knew
were children of workers
on his grandfather's farm.

~

It was a time a time, as a nine-year-old,
he learned to drive the gray Ford tractor,
a time along Georgia asphalt and dirt roads
red International Harvesters pulled harrows
and green John Deeres pulled hay bailers
field to field, farm to farm;
a time when pastel chenille bathrobes and bedspreads
were hung for sale on clotheslines
along U.S. 1 on the way to Florida,
motels flashed *whites only* in pink neon that matched
the plastic flamingos along their semi-circular driveways
and billboards demanded in gigantic letters:

IMPEACH EARL WARREN
CHIEF JUSTICE OF THE SUPREME COURT

~

It was a time of washing machines
on front porches in parts of town;
in other parts *colored* maids
hung laundry on backyard clotheslines,
polished silver and washed Wedgwood china;
a time when crosses were burned on top of Stone Mountain,
(owned by the Imperial Wizard of the KKK),
and burned on the front lawn of his parents' friend
Ralph McGill, publisher of the *Atlanta Constitution,*
because Mr. McGill supported desegregation.

It was a time he listened at night on his little beside radio
to *white radio,* WGUN and WSM-Nashville—Marty Robbins,
Earnest Tubb, Jerry Lee Lewis and Johnny Cash
and to *black radio,* WAOK—Howlin' Wolf,
Red Prysock, Piano Red, and Muddy Waters.
At sixteen he graduated from segregated Grady High School.

It was a time *coloreds* had to pay a poll tax and/or pass
a variety of *tests* if they dared try to register to vote—
One instruction read: *Spell* "backward," *forwards.*
A clerk might ask, *How many jelly beans
in that sealed jar on the desk?*

~

It was a time when *coloreds* were spit on for claiming
their place at Woolworth lunch counters in North Carolina,
when Freedom Riders were beaten, their buses burned in Alabama,
when civil rights workers Schwerner, Goodman and Chaney
were murdered, their bodies buried under a Mississippi dam,
a time when his maternal grandfather paced in the executive offices
of Rich's Department Store in Atlanta as *colored* students

marched outside and his mother refused to buy anything
in the store *until a colored woman doesn't have to go*
to the basement to use the bathroom or to get a bite to eat.

~

It was a time in the mid-1960s he went to law school in Chicago,
walked down a dark street into a hole-in-the-wall bar
to listen to BB King and Lucille—
the only white person in the audience;
a time when four Chicago police pointed guns up at him
as he stood on the roof of his townhouse watching
anti-Vietnam-war protesters gather
across the street in Lincoln Park—
the cops threatening him until he went inside.
A time when protesters were left bloodied
outside his front door.

It was the times he moved from Chicago to Atlanta
to Dallas to Minneapolis, counting among his friends
African American lawyers and laundry workers,
politicians, professors, and a police chief.

2.
November 4, 2008, eight-thirty in the morning.
He walks into a Minneapolis voting precinct
in the gym of a Catholic church,
takes his place in line—more than a hundred people
ahead of him, all upbeat, talking quietly;
he adjusts his hound's-tooth jacket and tan tie,
shifts his weight from foot to foot,
waits for over an hour until a poll worker signals
it is his time to vote.

In the voting booth, he pulls the curtain behind him,
picks up a newly sharpened No. 2 yellow pencil,
holds it between his thumb and forefinger
just like like he was taught in elementary school.

He stops. A question races through his mind—
How many white men in their sixties like me
will not vote for a man to become President
of the United States just because he is black?

He fills in the circle beside the name
Barack Hussein Obama,
votes the down-ballot races and initiatives,
opens the curtain, carries the completed
paper ballot to a locked gray metal box,
drops the ballot through the slit in the top of the box,
thanks the poll worker who hands him an *I Voted* sticker.

     My brother Daniel walks outside
     into the brisk Minnesota air
     and he begins to cry.

VII

~ need to find a Mason jar, poke holes in the lid ~

Apparently

I try to tell other people how to run their lives,
apparently
I don't think that's what I'm doing . . .
Have you tried. . . ? Why don't you. . . ?
If it was my choice . . .

which it wasn't this morning when I found a slug
in the downstairs bathroom
and had to pull out a large wad of toilet paper
to pick it up and flush it down the toilet
which I prayed didn't need the plunger today
though I admit to plunging into slug days—

unmade bed, lunch in pajamas,
and even whole slug seasons
not recorded in the Farmer's Almanac—
like the winter I let a friend's thirty-year-old maple bonsai die
and then let the palm tree he gave me die,
but, honestly, I don't let every plant die—

creeping raspberry creeps past the window,
through the screen and into the downstairs guest room.
One guest thought it was a thin green snake,
which is not likely considering my fear of snakes,
which my mother used to suggest was Freudian,
but I say *bullshit*! and having grown up on a dairy farm
I do know manure and should know how
to take care of animals, but Joe, my dog with allergies,
doesn't always get his weekly medical bath,
though for a couple of years I did give him a shot
once a week, and I still get weak in the knees

and loopy in the head after a second gin and tonic,
but in no way am I prepared to gin up the courage
to eat monkey brains or eels, no matter
how elegantly they may be flambéd in a pan

or the vintage of champagne poured into Waterford flute
    as Pan with his magic flute serenades a sylvan sunset.

Visitors

During construction of a new, smaller house a few years after my husband's death, I walked up the hill to the construction site and saw his name, *Howard*, and a drawing like Curious George, who had been a favorite of our children, writ large on a plywood sheet nailed over studs under the eaves twenty feet off the ground, only reachable with scaffolding—of which there was none.

A few days later, there appeared an enormous yellow outline of Mickey Mouse, one of Howard's favorites—Howard was buried in a Mickey Mouse tie—drawn on the black tar paper laid down on the topmost part of the roof before the shingles were nailed into place. There had been a rain the night before and no workmen since. The outline of Mickey remained for a few days, gradually fading until the shingles covered it.

Every now and then, ten years later, out of the corner of my eye, I see a wisp of translucent pale blue light slip past a corner inside the house.

Dead Body Parts

1.

I've just returned from picking up my neighbor Debbi, whose car was hit by an-
other car driven by a woman drifting across lanes of Holcomb Bridge Road near
Spalding Drive. While we waited for the police, we noticed that the drifting
woman, wearing skin-tight black leggings hardly appropriate for her body type
and furiously chewing gum, was gathering stuff from her car into a large garbage
bag and dumping the bag into the Dunkin' Donuts trash can across the parking
lot. Debbi shared these observations with the police, who inquired of the woman
what this was about. The woman explained, *I picked up my neighbor's garbage and
was getting rid of it in case there were dead body parts in the bag. I didn't want to be
caught with contraband when the police arrived.*

2.

This reminded me of the day a year or so ago when two police cars showed up in
our yard. I inquired if I could help. They pointed to a couple of twelve- or four-
teen-year-old boys in the backseat of one of the vehicles who had called the po-
lice to report: *We have found dead body parts in a wooden box on property by the
river.* The boys directed the police to our property.

The boys waited in the driveway with one cop while I got into the other police
car and guided the cop down a gravel road through the woods to the river. Right
there was an eight-foot by four-foot by four-foot wooden box sitting on a small
red trailer—a box we fill each July Fourth with two thousand pounds of block
and chopped ice and hundreds of pounds of chicken and baby back ribs, also a
keg or two of beer and Hershey bars for s'mores. Inside the box were a few of
the large, heavy brown bags used to carry chopped ice. The ice had long since
melted, but sure enough, in one bag were bones—chicken neck and back bones,
remains from the past July Fourth. Apparently the guest who had planned to
take them home and make stock forgot them. The boys were crestfallen. Their
reward—a lecture by the police about trespassing.

Fireflies

First fireflies of summer
light my way
down
the gravel road

one
then another
four more
a cluster high in a loblolly pine
three in the butterfly bush
a constellation
on the edge of the woods

I've lost count
need to find a Mason jar
poke holes in the lid
before my grandchildren
come to visit.

VIII

A LA MÉMOIRE DES ÉLÈVES DE CETTE ÉCOLE
DÉPORTÉS DE 1942 A 1944 PARCE QUE NÉS JUIFS,
VICTIMES INNOCENTES DE LA BARBARIE NAZIE
AVEC LA COMPLICITÉ DU GOUVERNEMENT DE VICHY.

ILS FURENT EXTERMINÉS DANS LES CAMPS DE LA MORT.
390 ENFANTS VIVAIENT DANS LE 19ème

9 NOVEMBRE 2002   NE LES OUBLIONS JAMAIS

~ pregnant with me as these children were being murdered ~

Memory & Complicity

Paris, April 2002

I stand in a line of mostly silent people
on the sidewalk beside the *Memorial de la Shoah*.
I am sixty years old; this is my first visit
to a Holocaust museum—that it is called
the *Memorial de la Shoah* makes it seem
less devastating than *Holocaust Museum*.

I pass through tall iron gates, a metal detector,
a handbag search and into a courtyard
flooded with Paris sunshine. At the opposite end,
a verdure cylinder the size of a small room,
embossed with names of concentration camps
—Birkenau, Bergen-Belsen, Buchenwald,
Dachau, Treblinka, Theresienstadt, Auschwitz—
To my left a garden of polished ten-foot high
stone walls inscribed with names and birth years
of seventy-six thousand French Jews murdered
at the hands of the Nazis,
murdered with the complicity
of the French government—
eleven thousand are children.

I caress the cool stone walls;
my fingers trace the letters and numbers.

~

On my walk to this place I'd stopped and read
a plaque beside the door of a school.

> *To the memory of the students of this school*
> *deported from 1942 to 1944 because of being born Jewish*
> *innocent victims of Nazi barbarity*
> *with the complicity of the government of Vichy.*
> *They were exterminated in the death camps.*
> *390 children who lived in the 19th arrondisment.*

9 November 2002/ We will never forget them.
I understood in that moment that my mother,
American for four generations,
Jewish for centuries, was pregnant with me
as these children were being murdered.

How much had she known of these murders
at quickening, my first kick?

~

I cross the courtyard, enter a building
with a forty-five-foot white stone façade,
walk down stairs into an exhibition hall—
glass cases full of photographs of strangers
who do not seem like strangers to me.
I touch the glass. My eyes settle on eyes,
cheekbones, lips, on diaries, letters, children's drawings.
I thumb through scraps of family histories
pieced together into tidy booklets by museum archivists.

What did my mother think
as my kick grew stronger against her ribs?
Or my father, born somewhere
along the Russian/Polish border
just before the century turned—
he never mentioned the name of his birthplace,
nor why his family came to America,
never mentioned this Holocaust in Europe.

I step into a U-shaped gallery, walls formed
by three blindingly back-lit glass panels.
On each panel, hundreds
of black-and-white snapshots of children—
school classes, sisters with matching bows in their hair,
boys cleaned and scrubbed for the photographer,
a naked baby lying on a blanket, staring at me.

My mother gave birth to me in Atlanta, Georgia,
sixteen days after the United States announced
that two million Jews had been murdered in Europe,
that five million more were in jeopardy.

I watch small video monitors—
naked bodies, only skin and bones are tossed into pits;
aging survivors give testimony in languages
I cannot translate but somehow understand.
I linger over cases with deportation lists,
well-worn identity cards stamped *JUIF,*
personal belongings—a penknife, a shirt, a dress,
a leather satchel, three faded cloth patches
each with a yellow Star of David—the patches all Jews,
including children, were required by the Nazis to wear in public.

> I remember my mother telling me
> that when she was pregnant with my younger brother,
> someone (I don't know who) asked her—
> *Why, in 1945, would you bring*
> *another Jewish child into this world?*
> (I don't know how she answered.)

I stand in a closet-like room, glass walls
between me and shelf after shelf, row after row
of long, narrow, blonde wooden boxes
jammed full of hand-written cards
with names and addresses of Jews catalogued
like books in the school library of my Georgia childhood.

> When I was ten years old, I watched from our car
> as Klansmen crossed Mt. Vernon Road
> near the Sandy Springs water tower—
> single file, dressed in white hoods and full Klan regalia,
> piling into the back of a large white box truck
> with a pull-down back door.

I dreamed for weeks they would come
in that white truck, take me and my family away.

I walk down a few more steps into a silent,
dimly lit room—a black marble Star of David,
five or six feet in diameter, hovers horizontally
a few inches above the floor. Beneath it,
a crypt filled with ashes—ashes from the sites
of concentration camps and the Warsaw ghetto.
I walk along the stone steps that circle the crypt,
recite the ancient mourner's prayer—
Y is-ga-dal v'yis-ka-dash sh'may ra-bo . . .

Step by step I climb the stairs
back up into the Paris April sunshine,
pass through the tall iron gates onto *rue Geoffroy-l'Asnier*,
walk down a few blocks to the river Seine
where old men smoking cigarettes
sit on benches under trees beginning to leaf,
car horns beep and newspapers blow into the street.

Along the Seine

It has been forty years since the summer
after my junior year in college
when I lived in Cluis in the middle of France
and sewed hats on a black Singer
treadle sewing machine
for the *Fetes et Jeux du Berry*—
monk skull caps, jaunty men's hats,
fine ladies' chapeaux, jester hats with tentacles and bells.
I slept in the tower of the *Mairie de Cluis*,
one tiny light on the winding stairwell,
an unlit two-seater outhouse off to the side of the tower.

It has been fifteen years since
I stood under the Eiffel Tower
in the December rain with my husband,
our daughters, aged fourteen and seventeen,
and our son, twenty, on holiday from Oxford.
We chanced upon an organist practicing
baroque melodies in Notre Dame
and ate at *Le Boeuf sur le Toit*—clams, oysters,
snails, and lobster on four-tiered ice-filled stands,
a pair of Russian wolfhounds stretched out
beside their owners at a nearby table.

It has been a day and a half since I left Atlanta
for a week-long writing workshop in Paris—
in my bag an English/French-French/English dictionary,
a Paris street map and a laptop computer.
Two hours since I waited alone
in a quiet line on the sidewalk beside
the *Memorial de la Shoah*—
passed through a metal detector
into a courtyard flooded with Paris sunshine.
Half an hour since
I walked out of the *Memorial de la Shoah*,
and down to the Seine

the *Memorial* at my back,
Notre Dame across the river.
Trees beginning to bud green.
Impatient car horns.
Cigarette smoke in the air.

      Bergen-Belsen, Buchenwald

I walk unhurried along the Seine,
motorcycles zip between cars,
women's heels click on the street,
dogs on leashes defecate
as owners pretend not to notice.
I pass the green wrought-iron railings
of the Pont d'Arcole, over which
the first French armored division arrived
during the 1944 Liberation of Paris,
turn up *rue du Renard,*
pass the Hôtel de Ville, Paris's city hall,
stop at a café across from the Musée Pompidou—
its post modern exoskeleton of red and blue and green steel
a stark contrast to the French Renaissance Hôtel de Ville.
I order *pain au chocolat* and *café decaf* at the bar,
wait at a small round sidewalk table
with a dirty ashtray.

      Dachau

I imagine my mother, a young woman
studying at the Sorbonne in 1928,
café au lait with studies in the morning,
in the Louvre, how she'd have looked up
a long flight of stairs and seen for the first time
the Winged Victory of Samothrace;
her comings and goings through
the soaring glass and iron hall of the Gare du Nord,
vin rouge ordinaire with friends in the evening,
her flirtations in Montmartre night clubs,

picnics of *baguettes et fromage* along the Seine
under trees leafing out now—
but they were still young then,
the trees and my mother,
her dark hair parted in the middle,
pulled into a small bun at the nape of her neck,
softened over her ears, her brown eyes intense,
her perfectly accented Parisian French.

Treblinka

My mother left Paris in the spring of 1929,
nineteen years old;
eleven years later, June 1940,
Nazi troop trains
pull into the Gare du Nord,
disgorge German soldiers
through its Beaux Arts façade with orders
(and the collaboration of the Vichy government)
to track down and catalog every Jew in Paris—
every Jewish man, woman, and child.

Five months later, my mother gives birth
in Washington, D.C. to her first child, my brother.

Theresienstadt

Summer 1942; my mother is thirty-three.
I have a snapshot of my her pregnant with me,
my brother, nearly two, clinging to her hem,
my grandmother and great-grandmother alongside her—
four generations of American-born Jews
smiling in the Georgia sunshine of my grandparents' garden
as nearly 5,000 miles away in Paris,
the Nazis prepare to launch Operation Spring Breeze—
       13,152 Parisian Jews will be arrested
         4,115 of them children

Five months later in December I am born.

Auschwitz

~

I sip my coffee;
sweet flaky pastry bits of *pain chocolat*
spill through my fingers.
Shadows lengthen across the round table.
Abandoned copies of *Le Monde*
blow to the ground.

I finish my coffee, cold by now,
finger Euro coins in my pocket,
put a few on the table beside
the slip of paper that is my bill.
I step to the curb, check my map.

      I can almost hear Nazi jackboots
      marching through the cobblestone streets.

Anthem

Inspired by the Winged Victory of Samothrace—190 BC

She is olive-skinned from Spain
high-yellow from Georgia
red from the pueblos
ochre from Thailand
She is blue-black from Nigeria

She is marble white from the isle of Paros.

She is dressed in saffron silk
in polyester pastel
in a cap and gown
a wedding gown
a night gown

She is dressed in folds of fabric falling to her feet.

She is Semitic
Caucasian
African
She is Mayan
Persian

She is Greek.

She is an entrepreneur
an engineer
an exotic dancer
a midwife
She is a warrior

She is winged.

She stands at a podium in Seneca Falls
over a crib in Helena

with scissors in a Kentucky beauty shop
She stands for election
stands at a bus stop in Birmingham

She is more than two thousand years old.

She bakes bread
hauls water and firewood
She bleeds
She splints hearts
lays rosemary on gravestones

*She stands atop a staircase in the Louvre—
sea winds lifting her wings behind her.*

The Maestro Plays My Mother's Piano

A miscellany of chairs is crammed together
in our living room—wooden and wrought iron ones,
dining room and kitchen ones, my great-grandfather's
oversized barrel-back tapestry-covered chair.
In the corner a Steinway ebony baby grand piano,
lid half-opened, all eighty-eight keys tuned yesterday,
my mother's piano.

In the living room and spilling out into an August evening
on the screened-in porch—a symphony conductor, musicians,
music patrons, an ethicist, an intellectual property rights attorney.
Near the piano a rabbi holds the chair for an older woman—
pewter silk jacket/blouse with see-through sleeves
over a black dress, décolleté setting off a necklace
of gold rectangles. Shiny silver-white hair falling
to just above her shoulders held loosely from her face
with a headband. Clear skin, intense dark eyes
behind large, slightly tinted glasses.

~

Italian Maestro Francesco Lotoro
takes his seat on the black piano bench—
light blue open-collared shirt slightly un-tucked under
a black suit, mid-forties, wavy black hair thinning in the front
combed perhaps with his fingers, black rimmed glasses,
short beard and moustache. He nods shyly towards the guests,
leans over the keyboard and begins to play—
to play music he has tracked down
over the course of more than two decades
in a dozen countries—
sheets and scraps of paper in archives,
old bookshops and government records,
manuscripts and diaries
in forgotten drawers and cabinets of owners
willing to share these fragments of family history,

one anecdotal story to the next,
new clues to dead ends—
an archive of more than four thousand pieces of music
composed in the concentration camps and prisons of the Nazis—

composed in Westerbork—
I Love You (Ich Liebe Dich) by Willy Rosen,
a German singer, pianist, and composer
who fled to the Netherlands, was captured
and sent to Westerbork, where he was required
by the Nazis to write and stage cabaret performances.

composed in Riga—
Railway Song (Reischsbahlied)
by Ljowa Berniker, a nineteen-year-old
Lithuanian Jew. The Maestro explains
how Berniker's syncopated rhythm belies
lyrics describing conditions in the camp.

composed in Buchenwald—
A Night of Prayer (Noche del Plegaria) by Jozef Kropinski,
a Polish resistance fighter and violinist whose lyrics include:
> *In Buchenwald, the birch trees rustle sadly,*
> *as my heart sways languishing in woe.*
Kropinski wrote some three hundred quartets, songs,
piano and orchestra scores at night in the *pathology lab*
surrounded by mutilated cadavers of fellow prisoners.

More guests arrive. Bedroom chairs are squeezed in.
The Maestro bends into the piano, plays waltzes, tangos,
folk songs, tunes composed without certain notes because
pianos in the camps often lacked a full complement
of eighty-eight keys, plays melodies written for a limited number
of instruments because those were the only ones available.

Czech composer Rudolf Karel completed a *Nonet*
for nine instruments which the Maestro considers
like a telegraph— di-di-ti-ti di-di-ti-ti—
and at a certain moment imagine this is a Morse code.

Karel composed a five-act opera on toilet paper. Guards
allowed him extra toilet paper because he had dysentery.
He completed an upbeat *Prisoners' March* four days
before being shipped from Theresienstadt to his death at Auschwitz.

The Maestro shares stories of the Ghetto Swingers,
a jazz band in Theresienstadt, a *show camp*
where Red Cross officials were shown *how well* Jews were treated—
but were neither told Jewish musicians were forced to compose
and perform orchestral concerts and cabarets for Nazi officers,
nor of the train from Theresienstadt to Auschwitz.

      Austrian Viktor Ullman, a student of Arnold Schoenberg,
      wrote of making art in the camps—
            Our endeavor with respect to arts
            was commensurate with our will to live.
      Before his transfer from Theresienstadt to his death at Auschwitz,
      Ullman wrote some of twenty compositions — sonatas, lieder,
      orchestral pieces, and an opera.

The room is still. Wine glasses, empty.
The Maestro looks up, hands resting in his lap,
explains that Jewish Italian boxer Anticoli scribbled
the lyrics to *Star of the Port (Stella del Porto)*
on the wall of his Nazi prison cell. Describes tracking down
a very old woman still living near the former prison who,
in a frail voice, sang him the melody
four times over the telephone while I transcribed it.
He plays and sings a few bars.

The Maestro leans down to the piano keys,
plays lullabies composed in and sung to children
in the camps. I stand on the porch next to the conductor,
whisper to him the realization that my mother was pregnant
with me when these lullabies were written.
The Maestro is playing them on my mother's piano—
the piano on which she played children's songs

for my brothers and me, played Beethoven *Sonatas*
and Schumann's *Scenes from Childhood* we could hear
at night after we had gone to bed.

～

The Maestro stands up from the piano bench,
bows slightly, acknowledging the silence in the room.
I make my way through emptying chairs
to the woman in the low-cut blouse and gold necklace.
She looks hard into my eyes, takes both my hands in hers,
squeezes tightly—
>   *I was young and blonde and good-looking.*
>   *In the camps they tried to make us feel like rats,*
>   *like rats in a sewer, but we wouldn't let them.*
>   *Like rats. On the train I was able to use my looks*
>   *to distract the Nazi soldiers. I jumped*
>   *from the moving train into a field—and lived.*

She asks for another glass of Cabernet.
I take a photograph of her sitting with the Maestro
near my mother's piano.

～

Chairs askew. Living room empty.
Dessert dishes scattered. The piano lid still open.
My mother's music books on shelves nearby—
among them Bach's *Well-Tempered Clavier*
and *The Fireside Book of Folk Songs* from which
my brothers and I learned *Cockles and Mussels*
and *Go Down Moses*. On the shelves, as well,
a song book I bought when my children were young—
Lullabies and Night Songs illustrated by Maurice Sendak
whose own childhood in Brooklyn had been haunted
by the sobs of his Polish-born parents as news arrived
of the deaths of extended family at the hands of the Nazis.

Hush little baby, don't say a word
Mama's goin' to buy you a mockin' bird—

I sink down into my great-grandfather's barrel-back chair;
cicadas and tree frogs serenade just off the porch;
barred owls call to one another from the next hill.
    Somewhere far away a dog barks.

EPILOGUE

~ run barefoot in summer rain ~

Updates From the Meadow

1.
Brilliant yellow dandelions
near the bridge over Buck Creek
where it flows into the Chattahoochee

2.
Morels
in the damp edge
of the creek
clutch of seven Canada Goose eggs
poison ivy

3.
My old dog Pyramus
trotting proudly
head high
carrying the saddle and two bloody
hind legs of a deer

4.
Remnants of an old creek bridge
three thirty-six-inch corrugated steel pipes
askew
blanketed in a tumble of wild white roses

5.
Thin pillar of gray smoke
climbing from logs left smoldering
in a ring of concrete blocks
arranged by trespassers

6.
Sweet perfume
of honeysuckle
steady hum
of a beehive

7.

Dog Joe shivering heavily
looking skyward
watching a contrail grow
looking down then back up
expecting it to be gone

8.

Nine dead baby possums
in the middle of the meadow
one intense purple violet

Prayer

Oh Lord
let me be calm
silent as the dusk of a pine forest
let me lose fear

Oh Lord
comfort the cedar waxwings
gorging on cotoneaster berries
too drunk to fly
crashing into my windows
yellow bodies and red wing tips
stilled on the ground

Oh Lord
let go the frown
between my eyes
give my old dog Joe
ease as he tries to stand

Oh Lord
of births and beheadings
(for if you are there, you must be God of both)
put your thumb on the scales
of new stars
. and the air we breathe

Oh Lord
let my daughter's daughter
about to be born
run barefoot in summer rain
bits of fresh cut grass
sticking between her toes.

Notes

pp. 43–44 (Next to last stanza of 4400 Loblolly) _Shiva_ is the week long period of mourning following a loved one's death. Family members traditionally "sit" at home to receive visitors. _Y is-ga-dal v'yis-ka-dash sh'may ra-bo. . ._ from _Yizkor_, the Jewish Mourner's prayer. Translation: _Magnified and sanctified be the great name of God..._

p. 89 (beginning of Without Sanctuary) The lyrics at the beginning of each section of Without Sanctuary are from "Strange Fruit," music and lyrics written in 1937 by Abel Meeropol—a white Jewish teacher, poet, and composer, horrified by a 1930 photograph of a double lynching in Indiana which sold thousands of copies as postcards.

The descriptions of specific postcards in this poem are mine and come from studying the postcards and background information about each one in the exhibit and on the Without Sanctuary website. Direct quotes are in italics and sources identified. The Without Sanctuary collection is held at the Museum of Civil and Human Rights in Atlanta, Georgia.

p. 109 (VIII) One of the plaques placed in recent years on schools in Paris honoring children who attended that school and were murdered by the Nazis because they were Jewish. Often bouquets of flowers are left nearby. Translation:

> _To the memory of the students of this school_
> _deported from 1942 to 1944 because of being born Jewish,_
> _innocent victims of Nazi barbarity_
> _with the complicity of the government of Vichy._
> _They were exterminated in the death camps._
> _390 children who lived in the 19th arrisdonment_
> _9 November 2002/ We will never forget them._

p. 111 _(first page of Memory & Complicity) Shoah._ Hebrew word meaning _catastrophe,_ denoting the catastrophic destruction of European Jewry during World War II.

PHOTOGRAPHS

The Dean House. p. 1

Daniel, Eve, and Nathan Parker. p. 5

Joshua, Rebecca, and Judith Hoffman. p. 27

AIDS Memorial Quilt with "Think of Me" panel honoring John Brownfield. p. 55

Neely Farm dairy cattle on newly terraced hills. p. 65

Geraniums. p. 78

Greyhound rest stop between Louisville, Kentucky and Nashville, Tennessee. Photographer: Esther Bubley. Farm Security Administration, Library of Congress Collection. p. 87

Fireflies in a Mason jar. p. 101

One of the plaques placed near doors of Paris schools honoring Jewish children who attended that school and were murdered by the Nazis. p. 109

Grandchildren. p. 126

Acknowledgments

Memory & Complicity could not have been possible without my brothers Nathan and Daniel Parker always ready and patient to share their recollections and to correct mine, without the pride and teasing of my children Judith Hoffman, Rebecca Acheson and Joshua Hoffman, especially the stories of their father Howard Hoffman. This work would have never found its way without Ellen Hinsey who first convinced me that my stories as a white, southern, Jewish, Smith College educated woman (of a certain age) mattered, without Jamil Zainaldin who taught me to value these stories in the broader context of southern culture and history, and without Cecilia Woloch, a relentless and unflinching teacher and mentor, who cut me no slack and celebrated when I nailed a poem. To so many of you who have read versions of these poems along the way, I thank you for your willingness to indulge me with your time and wisdom. *Memory & Complicity* would have remained scattered in bits and pieces in my mind and on my desk without Sal Brownfield's unwavering belief in me as a poet and in the power of the arts, indeed of my stories, to engage the world in unique ways with unexpected clarity. I am honored that his drawing of an *Old Tree* graces the cover of this book.

The following poems have appeared in previous versions:

In *Red Clay,* Finishing Line Press 2010: Circles in the Sky, Red Clay, Miss Lizzie's Kitchen, He Taught them How to Shovel, 4400 Loblolly Trail, Requiem, Rachel's Pot

In *The Saporta Report,* October 12, 2015: The Yellow Dress

In *SHE,* Five Oaks Press 2016: She-Part One, Jumping Off the Refrigerator, She-Part Two, Arabia Mountain, Prayer

The Author

Eve Hoffman loves dirt roads and Guernsey cream. She's been called a provoca-
teur and has been honored by her alma mater, Smith College, as a *Remarkable
Woman* and by *Georgia Trend* as one of a hundred influential people in the state.
Her previous books include poetry chapbooks *Red Clay* and *SHE* and her inter-
views with twenty-one models impacted by breast cancer accompanying Sal
Brownfield's paintings in *A Celebration of Healing*. She lives in the woods by the
Chattahoochee River with artist Sal Brownfield.